A child of the 1940s, Lesley was removed from school against her wishes and sent to work to support her family, but she never forgot her childhood dream of becoming a pilot.

While working six days a week and looking after her own family, Lesley used her precious nights and Sundays to study and take lessons. At the age of 35, flying became her escape and her one true love. Estrangement from her husband and children was the price she paid to touch the clouds.

With a flying career spanning 40 years from her first lesson to her retirement at 73 as Australia's oldest female pilot, in *Up There*, Lesley shares her bigger-than-life story with characteristic honesty and irreverence.

Lovers, friends and enemies form the amazing array of characters that populate Lesley's life as she recounts her memories of living and flying in over 15 countries. Working for the Red Cross and United Nations in regions where war and civil unrest make daily life dangerous, she recalls her hair-raising African adventures – from being shot at mid-air in Angolan skies to fending off an attempted robbery in its streets.

A straight-shooting Australian working in a male-dominated industry, Lesley has always fought against injustice with humour, resilience and compassion. Her no-nonsense stance has occasionally cost her jobs and relationships, but she has gained a wealth of life lessons and sensational stories that will delight the next generation of pilots and adventurers alike.

I would like to dedicate this book to my many friends, colleagues and students who gave me permission to tell their stories even when it was not always complimentary.

My apologies to many not mentioned, remember I hold you all in my heart. Special thanks to the Jones family, Hayden, Heather, Brendan and Rory. As well as my Swedish friends – those very special three sisters.

Lesley Crowther-Scott

UP THERE

AUSTIN MACAULEY PUBLISHERS™

LONDON • CAMBRIDGE • NEW YORK • SHARJAH

A CIP catalogue record for this title is available from the British Library.

ISBN 9781398433410 (Paperback)
ISBN 9781398434042 (ePub e-book)

www.austinmacauley.com

First Published (2020)
Austin Macauley Publishers Ltd
25 Canada Square
Canary Wharf
London
E14 5LQ

Thank you to Shelley Hamer for your support and help in editing and making sense of my ramblings, Sebastiaan Theelen for checking my technical knowledge, and Greg Sheehy and Margaret Anne Morris for pushing me to put my story on paper.

Prologue

Aviation is an escape.
Aviation was my escape,
Soaring beyond dreams.
The atmosphere is so much lighter up there.
It is the place I never wish to leave; a place to stay forever.
Airborne forever, was and still is my ideal.
Is it because I cannot deal with life on earth?
There is not as much debris up there.
At ground level atmosphere is so heavy.
Energy at ground level is almost unbearable.
The aircraft I flew was a Twin Otter.
It is possible to open a cockpit window at altitude, as the Otter is an unpressurised aircraft. You can stick your hand out of the window and feel the clouds.
The clouds are always wet; visible moisture.
Like our tears, water that can be seen.
My life took a turn for adventure when I lost everything I held dear.
When people lose everything they care about, they tend to take risks that the average human being would not take.
We are not different from our fellow humans, we just no longer have anything to protect and keep safe, which leads us to take more risks. These risks always lead to adventure.

Chapter 1
Pre-Flight Briefing

Gunfire! When you first hear it, shocks you! Where is it coming from? Shit scared! Frantically searching for the source. Realising that it is not aimed at you and it is just people letting off steam, you relax, become complacent. Finally, you get used to the noise, the gunfire and life in places like Angola, Burundi, South Africa, Uganda and other developing countries. While out shopping, guards holding AK47s is a way of life. But constantly living life aware that at any time you may be target practice, causes stress, especially with a rotating roster of eight weeks on duty and four weeks off.

Corruption is rife and you quickly realise that while there are some good police, most are dishonest and you are as much at threat from them as you are with the general public. Living like this constantly makes you more accepting of your own mortality. You get used to it and the gunfire and noise are just a part of life.

At one stage, I could not go to sleep unless I could hear gunfire. When guns are pointed directly at you; your knees knock. One day, we were approaching Bujumbura—the main airport in Burundi—and we could see pipes that looked like a pipe organ, swivel in our direction. Greg my first officer (FO) yelled "Rocket launcher!" For immediate avoidance, we dropped below the approach path quickly. Both sides of the approach path to the runway had long grass at least two metres high, so we dropped down abruptly in the hope that the long grass would obscure our flight path from the soldiers. I have no idea if it worked but we landed and taxied far too fast into one of the bays of the airport terminal building.

While I closed the aircraft down, Greg undid his seat belt and raced through the cabin to open the entry door at the rear of the aircraft and hurry the passengers out.

The United Nations' representative ran to the aircraft asking, "What are you doing here?"

"What do you mean? We are supposed to be here."

"Didn't you get our message?"

"What message?"

"We told Ngozi Airport to keep you there. We have been under attack for two hours! Leave the aircraft and get inside."

We left all the luggage and cargo behind and took refuge in the terminal.

As quickly as it began, it was all over. We jumped in the four-wheel drive and headed home.

Such is life, working for the Red Cross and the United Nations. I worked for the South African company that held the contracts for these two organisations. However, they also held contracts with oil companies and I spent time in Algeria flying out to the Sahara along with my crew. We marvelled at the haboobs, which are gigantic sandstorms. We landed at the flattest place on earth, also in Algeria at a place called Reg, in the Red Sahara.

While I never made it into the majors, I would not change a minute of my aviation career. I have lived and worked in fifteen countries and travelled to over fifty. I have been shot at, suffered an engine failure, and had an engine shot out, but all the while I have had the unique experience of being able to touch the clouds.

I can touch clouds because I was lucky enough to pursue a career that occasionally put me in harm's way, but gave me immense satisfaction and fulfilment.

Touching a cloud gives me contact with something ethereal—while it doesn't give the warmth of love or physical contact, it gives me the feeling of being special, something that is free and priceless.

A Twin Otter is a very old unpressurised aircraft and sometimes the cockpit window slowly opens because things no longer fit as tightly as they should. The windows can be pulled up or pushed open during flight. At about 10,000 feet there is lots of cloud build up. I noticed that the engine noise had become louder and began to search for the noise when we realised that my window had slightly dropped down from the fully closed position. I decided to open it a little more to put my hand out into the airflow and touch the clouds.

Why did I touch a cloud? Because touching a cloud touches some part of me.

Which came first, the chicken or the egg? My flying gave me the ability to touch a cloud, but touching a cloud is the reason I fly.

I guess it sounds silly, but it gives me a sense of proportion and reminds me how infinitesimal I am and how human beings are such a small part of the universe. Touching a cloud is something very special to me, something wonderful.

I know it is just moisture and your hand feels wet, damp, and cold. Cloud is warmer than the air around it and so the moisture in the air condenses, cloud forms because of the difference between the temperature of the air in the cloud and the surrounding air. But here at ten thousand feet, I can put my hand into the cloud and feel at absolute peace.

I know for those who can't fly that this must seem out of reach, but it is possible to touch a cloud at ground level although the idea for me isn't as fulfilling. We have all experienced cloud at ground level as fog. Cloud is just visible moisture, but it seems different to be able to stick your hand into thick cumulus. It always makes the hairs on the back of my neck stand on end with the magic of it.

It makes me feel connected to the universe, the natural world. We all need to feel connected.

I have no connection with my family and flying makes me feel connected to my greater self.

I decided to learn to fly after two major events in my life.

***

I had an early cancer and then I survived a serious car accident. These two events changed my thinking and were the best things that have ever happened to me. They made me take a look at life; what is it all about?

Despite the many hardships I have endured in my life, my outlook is positive because I have worked in something I am passionate about, flying.

My earliest memories are of flying, even when recalling simple things like helping my mother by hanging out the washing. We lived in Melbourne, on the extended runway centreline of Essendon Airport, and aircraft often operated overhead. I remember when I was about seven years old, I looked up to see an aircraft overhead. It was a Douglas DC3—a tail dragger. As I looked up in awe of this wonderful sight, I remarked to my mother, that that is what I wanted to do. Fly something like that. Years later, I finally did. Once, when flying in Sweden my FO invited me to stay at his home in Stockholm, and that weekend his old flying club had arranged for three DC3s to take members of the club to the Island of Gotland. Visby is the seat of Gotland and the major town of this area. They were holding a medieval weekend. Would I like to go? "Yes," said I. So, here I was on an old DC3, which had been in the Queen's Flight and even had the original crockery that had been used to serve royalty on board. The captain of the DC3 invited me to the cockpit. To say I flew it is an exaggeration, as I only flew it at height, I did not land it. I thoroughly enjoyed the weekend.

At the medieval fair they had public baths with big wooden tubs, filled with adults in swimwear. One rather inebriated gentleman decided to get in on the action and divested himself of all his clothes, as mothers discreetly ushered their children away. Starkers is what we would call it in Oz. Greatly amused, we wondered how the ladies of the bath would handle this little display and (yes it was not the proverbial six inches). Instead of continuing to supply warm water on this chilly day, with much laughter, they suddenly began adding cold water with some ice, provided by the local stallholders. The gentleman in the tub seemed suddenly shocked into sobriety and exited the tub post-haste, with much cheering and many catcalls about the effect the cold had on his genitals.

***

I shall try to keep things chronological, dealing with the countries I ended up in and the events as they happened but as I write one thing, it tends to stir new memories. So, forgive me if it sometimes seems like rambling.

From my first take-off, I can still remember the intake of breath that I took as the wheels left the ground. All these years later, I still get that buzz. Not so much from the take-off, but from the challenge in bad weather and the thrill when I taxi in, having matched my skills against the elements once again, and won.

My first landing on snow, dealing with ice, different airspaces—all had their own challenges. As I travelled, I had to learn not only to deal with different weather patterns, but also the difficulties presented by new cultures, cuisines and living arrangements. I learned to listen to local pilots as they often had experience in areas I didn't, and were worth listening to. I learned to shut my mouth and open my ears.

***

As I got older, I learnt more about how natural events such as sandstorms and fog worked, and how to consider them in my flight planning. If a forecast said fog, my attention immediately went to the percentage chance of that fog—the split between the temperature and the dew-point—put together, these gave you an idea of how likely it was that the fog would need to be a consideration.

As we hung the washing out, the sheets and towels flapped in the wind, drying quickly with the effect of sun and wind. Never did I dream at this age how the wind would come to factor to such an extent later in my life. Drift X-track error, track made good and so it went. Tailwinds are always a benefit to estimated time of arrival, with headwinds slowing things down, as usual.

I learnt to tell wind direction by looking at the waves; as the wave breaks there is a froth that forms and a lace-type pattern flows back from the top of the wave—that is the exact direction that the wind is coming from.

In Vanuatu, a gentleman had asked if he could sit next to me as we flew single pilot there with a special dispensation. He was telling me that he had come to erect windsocks on all the strips. I think he expected me to be impressed and grateful, but Vanuatu is made up of 88 islands, and we spent much of our flight time over water. Therefore the pilots operating in this area already have the runway direction sorted by the time they hit the circuit. When I explained to this gentleman how we did it, he definitely seemed deflated.

I never thought I would achieve my dream of flying. My remarks to my mother as we hung the washing out, were the remarks of a dreamer, while her reply was from someone who had never dreamed. I was told not to be stupid—women don't fly. I learnt to dream by listening to people who even then, were the pioneers, some of whom, as I got older, I was lucky enough to meet, such as Freda Thompson (an Australian woman who flew solo from the UK, arriving in Darwin in 1937). There is a derby in her honour—The Freda Thompson Aerial Derby, held early each year in Melbourne.

In the early days of my learning to fly, Nancy Bird Walton gave an inspiring talk, telling the story of how they used to fly out of Sydney before they had 'real' weather reporting. They would ring up someone they knew at Katoomba, in the Blue Mountains of New South Wales (near the famous rock formation, the Three

Sisters). She told of flying in visibility so bad that she was flying along a railway track when low and, behold, right in front of her was a tunnel. Yes, she was nearly at ground level. With sudden power and climb, she just cleared the top of the tunnel. She then, having decided perhaps it was not safe to continue, put down in a farmer's field. She knocked on his door, was fed and shown to the guest room by the farmer's wife and next morning, with the weather clearing, the farmer and his workers helped move the Tiger Moth to the road, where she took off and continued the journey. What an amazing woman!

I have touched clouds; literally. I have seen the wonders of the world, the aurora borealis, and the haboobs in the Sahara; I have flown around the Pacific Islands and lived amongst many different yet beautiful people.

What a blast. Where did it all begin? Or perhaps I should say, why did it begin? For something new to begin, there always has to be an ending.

The end of my marriage was also my beginning. My husband asked me to decide between him and aviation. We had been married for 24 years and my children were all grown, so my answer was immediate—aviation. I have often described him as 'dead shit boring!' There was no way I was going to miss out on my dream. This reaction was received with shock and everyone I knew took it badly. However my children were getting married and living their own lives and I felt I had done my job by giving them the best education I could. I loved my children with every fibre of my body but unfortunately, I have never been forgiven, and to this day, I have no contact with them. So having lost everything I held dear, I threw caution to the wind and set about getting back on my feet. I did not have enough money for a new home, furniture etc. So I decided to sell the only commodity I had—my experience as a pilot. I applied for jobs anywhere and everywhere. My first tentative forays were still within Australia, and I ended up flying in Port Hedland. To best describe where it is, think of Australia as a rabbit with Cape York being the rabbit's ears. Port Hedland, which is located in Western Australia, is roughly where you would find the arsehole of the rabbit. Remote and featureless until your eyes adjust to the different landscape.

As a flying instructor in Melbourne, I was used to instructing in what is basically an amphitheatre, with the Dandenong Mountains, Mt Macedon and the Grampians surrounding the city and bay area. I was now faced with a hill of 200 feet (yes, in aviation height is still given in feet). At first, my eyes just did not 'see' this molehill, however, after a couple of weeks this molehill stood out like 'dogs balls' in the surrounding flat landscape. It was in this area that I had my first real engine failure.

Even though I haven't lived there for many years, I still think of Melbourne as home, and it is only since I have retired that my visits are no longer yearly. I still pop in when I can and see ex-colleagues, bosses and a few lovers that are still friends and often have a laugh. I never miss calling in on one of my favourite men—a gentleman called Steve Pearce who, in my opinion, is the best instrument-rating instructor in Australia. This unassuming man is totally aviation. When I last asked, which is probably about ten years ago, he had some 28000 hours and flies many different aircraft. Steve is the true professional and seems to work on the principle: if you can't say something nice, don't say anything, and I am proud to call this man my friend.

Never, during my short visits to Melbourne for license and rating renewals every year, did I try to see family, as they had made it perfectly clear I was not welcome. I stay well away from the areas where my family live and spend my time catching up with old friends.

My best girlfriend lives in Melbourne and she is married now, to a man I taught crosswind landings to; he now flies for a Hong Kong-based carrier. It is strange that many women taught young men to a level that was accepted by airlines, but we were never accepted until Debbie Lawrie took on Ansett Airlines in 1979. Debbie did my night rating and she deserved to be accepted.

In my experience, male crews never had a problem flying with women. We were welcomed into the cockpit by male colleagues. When Debbie Lawrie was cleared for line flying, I believe there was a welcome notice on the cockpit door. The word 'cockpit' was scribbled out and replaced with 'Box Office'; typical crew humour.

I am not, and never have been, a 'women's libber' and I think political correctness is a load of garbage and to blame for so much wrong in our society. I have always just done what I wanted to. Yes, people have said no to me and I have been knocked back for jobs, but my view was that the dickhead just missed out on a bloody good pilot. I must admit I did fight hard, on looking back, I think I was sometimes an obnoxious, loud-mouthed female that swore like a trooper and still does. But I could fly. I won prizes for handling and was often told I was in the top 2% of handlers. Any rejection just made me try harder.

Chapter 2
Discrimination

While I hear women cry discrimination, I personally received a lot of support from the men I worked with. The accepted wisdom was that we had to be twice as good to be recognised as half as good, but I didn't care; I was flying.

I went to a women pilots' meeting in 2013 where I heard a female air force pilot talk about 'placenta brain' (hormones running riot). I nearly fell off my chair. She said the Airforce just have to realise that women suffer this. My answer to that is: She should have been grounded—if you cannot fly then you should be on leave without pay. You are paid to fly aircraft so if you cannot do the job then—good-bye.

I had another lady who said, "I am having a mental health day."

I said, "You are grounded, as mental health is not a 'day thing', it is an ongoing health concern." Why should any company hand a multi-million-dollar aircraft over to a person who has mental health problems, just for a day? If you feel you have mental health problems then declare it, but not for the want of a day off. I read an article that said placenta brain DOES NOT exist. Many women suffer from postnatal depression, so don't cheapen it by calling it placenta brain. Declare it! By keeping yourself safe, you keep your passengers safe. If you cannot do the job, you shouldn't be in the cockpit.

You talk about discrimination, well, men cannot claim placenta brain, and it is equal work for equal pay. That is what they have maternity leave for.

***

While it hasn't happened to me, there are women who have been subjected to discrimination and sexual harassment. A young lady I know was a new Grade 3 instructor, and applying for a position, arrived in uniform carrying her licence and medical, plus references. She proudly handed over her paperwork, the chief flying instructor (CFI) undid his fly and exposed himself and said, "Suck on this and the job's yours." Thank god the young woman left and reported him to the police. This should never happen but there are people out there who do and will.

One day, a new female pilot turned up at work and said, "I will be missing for a couple of days, as I have an interview with Qantas." Apart from being surprised as she had only just started, I said "Okay, well, good luck." She was successful, but as I congratulated her, she let slip she had turned up to interview without her licence, medical references or ratings. Your ratings explain aircraft types you are certified to fly, instrument ratings and renewals. All evidence of experience is kept in your licence. She had gone empty-handed and was still employed by this company. I would bet a year's salary that if a man had done that, he would not have been hired. But with the quota system, they don't have to be professional, or efficient, they just have to turn up. Now, how is this for a scary thought? She may be the pilot on your next flight. My mind boggles when I think of how they could have offered employment to such a dunderhead.

***

I was in Cairns with a broken ankle when a lass working with the same company started talking about discrimination. I said, I didn't think I had been discriminated against, however over the next few days we continued talking and as I related a story, she stopped me and said, "Lesley, that is discrimination." As I thought about it, I had to admit that yes, it was. But at the time I was so busy trying to prove myself, head down, bum up, I didn't even notice. If it wasn't for the efforts of women like me, the young women of today would not have made it. If we had been the strident do-gooders of today, then we would never have achieved what the young women of today take for granted and still bitch about.

I do object to positive discrimination; for example, I know that one of the early female Qantas pilots was given an extra chance to pass her flight assessment. Men are given two attempts, but she needed three. That is wrong; equal work means you do the job to the same standard as expected in the same amount of tries—zero favours. I had taught crosswind landings to this particular lady and she did not do them well. When I said they are not good enough she shrugged her shoulders said, "My Dad is a VIP, we have enough pull to get me in to any company I want." I heard that in the end, she bent an aircraft (had an accident). I did not find that surprising, as she did it while flying with her father and they knowingly entered a thunderstorm.

***

Another time, my Australian renewal was due; it is not only flying we are tested on but also regulations. Basically regulations are the same everywhere but there are some small idiosyncrasies. I was checking my knowledge with a very experienced instructor when in walked this young pilot, who said, "You poor suckers, I don't have to bother with that. My Dad is a Qantas captain and I will get in without needing to do crap like that."

Well, as it turned out, Daddy couldn't hide the fact that sonny boy flew below the glide path on an Instrument Landing System (ILS) and killed his passengers. While we were studying, he was being given a 30-minute endorsement on a PA 31/350 known as a Piper Chieftain. These are beautiful aircraft but fast, therefore, reaction time must be quick, and scan must be quick. They need an experienced pilot.

The overconfidence of some young pilots is disproportionate to ability. The saying used to be that the most dangerous time in any pilot's flying is 100 hours, 300 Hours and 1000 hours. At 100 hours, they usually have their initial licence with restrictions removed. This means that they can venture from their training area associated with the aerodrome they are learning at. At 300 hours, they think they know it all, and at 1000 hours, they know they know it all. This kind of behaviour kills people. Usually, having survived incidents during the span of time to 1000 hours, they settle down and begin learning again. Not the book learning—the reality of staying alive.

People talk about the great responsibility of being a pilot and having all those lives sitting behind you. I must admit, I never once thought about those people; I thought about me—if I am safe, they are safe. Makes sense, doesn't it? I am not prepared to risk my life by taking on anything I can't handle, so by keeping me safe I keep you safe. That, after all, is the end result we all aim for. A standard is a standard and when the authority, the airline or the company plays favouritism to fill a quota then the end result is likely to be an accident or death.

***

Chapter 3
Me Too

As I write this, the ramifications of the 'me-too' campaign are still quite fresh. This sort of behaviour has been going on since women entered the workforce, not just actresses and actors but aviation too. We used to call those kind of leeches 'Captain Corridor' as they knocked their way down the corridor of where the crew was stationed that night. It used to be wheels up single, wheels down married. "Yippee! Here I come ladies!"

Back in the day, women got positions as FOs or captain on smaller aircraft in a process similar to the casting couch experience. Today, interviews are usually conducted by a panel. However, with smaller companies, it can still be just one-person interviewing, with occasionally horrifying outcomes, as happened with the Grade 3 applicant.

Struggling with language in some countries has also caused some really funny situations. Once in Dusseldorf, I had been sent down to refuel the aircraft and I had been directed on how to request the amount of fuel. I apparently did this reasonably well as the refueller continued to chat to me in German. In my attempt to be polite, I remarked, "Es ist heibes," which I thought meant, "The weather is hot." But somehow, I got it wrong and said, "Ich bin heib," which apparently means, "I am randy/sexy." Hence, I found myself fighting for my honour. Language, on more than one occasion, has been the cause for such hilarity. A misunderstanding in France saw our cabin crew, made up of some very pretty English girls, swimming topless. There was almost a riot at the local pool where many young men were visibly excited.

Chapter 4
Short Fuse

I had no intention of being an instructor; I was in my forties and didn't think anyone would want to learn off granny. I first started instructing at Moorabbin Airport, Melbourne. Next was Port Hedland in North Western Australia.

It was in these initial positions that I learnt my trade—how to impart knowledge with humour. People learn best in a happy atmosphere, there's no need for foot stomping and carry-on.

I quickly learnt that I had a short fuse, never for the student, but for the so-called professionals, who thought they were better, superior to their fellow man. I refuse to deal with bullshit—the drama queens, and emotional blackmail that people seem to feed off, was not for me. I tend to disperse with manipulators very quickly. This is the result of growing up with people who had diplomas in these traits, and marrying a manipulator. Now, I know that we all put on our pants one leg at a time—I've yet to meet someone who can levitate to do that. I became known for getting the job done with little fuss, no time for inefficiency or bullshit.

My flight crew licenses opened up the world for me. I was too old to fly the really big aircraft but having the licenses meant I was free to apply for positions all over the world. I ended up in the UK as an FO on the Viscount. This aircraft was considered to have the highest workload of all aircraft except the Belfast, which was not only much larger but had three crew in the cockpit. Someone I respect as an aviator with excellent knowledge of aircraft and systems, mentioned that these days, the old Viscount would be considered steam driven!

Cheeky bastard! They were beautiful to fly—just like an overgrown PA28 or Cherokee 6. A very forgiving aircraft, docile, lovely to handle, and without any nasty habits. Although one of my friends, who used to be my captain, is now quite deaf, as the Rolls Royce Dart engine cuts a line through your hearing. He was on them for seven years and, in one range, is quite hard of hearing. His wife and I quite often have a joke about his deafness in this range.

Chapter 5
The Beginning

When I was in my 30s, a girlfriend had suggested that I join her in going to university. I really didn't feel like doing that; I had become a TAB agent (an Australian betting shop) and in those days we received a commission. I was earning really good money so I decided to learn to fly, never for one-minute thinking I would become a professional.

I attended night classes for basic level aeronautical knowledge, meteorology, navigation, and flight planning, air law, principle of flights and aerodynamics.

Much later, I sat for the UK licence, which was considered at that time to be the most difficult licence in the world to obtain, not by attending class or a course, but by self-study, which was considered almost impossible. I actually got 100% for Performance A (an extremely difficult exam where the thickness of your pencil due to lines of graphs could be the difference between a pass and fail), and I was one of only five people who had achieved this mark at that time.

So, here I was working, attending class, and running a home, studying after everyone else had gone to bed. Imagine the look on my ex-husband's face when I walked in, and said, "You know those exams I sat last week? They were only at a private pilot level, but I passed them all."

Stunned, he said, "Well I guess there is nothing to stop you now." How right he was. There was nothing to stop me.

Chapter 6
Family

I must admit my family and my then husband made life as difficult as possible, however, this is not the place to get heavy. All of us have traumas in our lives, and I am no different. However, I did have one supporter—my dad.

My dad was working for Trans Australian Airlines as an aircraft welder. In those days they did not have the health and safety protection apparatus that they have now, so as Dad aged, he became extremely deaf.

Early in my training, he came flying with me and a girlfriend. As we were coming into Moorabbin Airport to land, we were on runway 22—a runway only used rarely and these days not at all, as the suburbs have come out to meet the aviation industry. This runway was used only when a major crosswind was blowing. I had been a bit slow to go solo as my instructor had forgotten to teach me about trim, (trim takes the load of the control column) as I struggled to hold the aircraft in the air (an impossible task unless you are built like King Kong). As I made this approach with my father on board, my girlfriend who was also a newly qualified pilot said, "Hey, that is one hell of a crosswind."

I remember laughing and saying, "You take the power off, it will come down, no worries." We landed and taxied off thinking no more about it.

I learnt much about how to do crosswind approaches right down the runway centreline. The next time my instructor demonstrated, and I saw him wind the trim wheel, I said "What are you doing?"

He said, "Have I forgotten to teach you about trim?" Once explained, I was solo 20 minutes later.

The following weekend, I visited my parents only to have my mother say that when she was telling Dad off the other day for tracking in mud, his response was, "I nearly died the other day, get off my back!" He was of course referring to my crosswind landing. I did laugh. As I said I was slow to go solo, but by the time I did there wasn't a landing scenario I hadn't experienced.

***

Some years later, I was working in Bunbury Western Australia, filling in for the chief pilot. He was a great guy but a little too amenable, and was being put under pressure by some of the locals. The boss knew I had a 'special way with fools and dickheads' and asked me to sort them out. I was there for four weeks and sure enough I had four altercations. The head of this little group was an old guy down from Serpentine, where there is an airfield seemingly governed by a sports aircraft builders club. He actually swaggered when he walked.

He saw I was about to go out flying, and told the 'little lady' that he thought it was beyond my capabilities. I had around 12500 hours at this time. I said "Say again." (Aviation for repeat.)

He said, "It's too much for you."

I said, "Hey, you just ground looped, I haven't yet—so please, explain!" (A ground loop in an aircraft is where a wing hits the ground or the nose of the aircraft ends up where the tail should be—it can demolish an aircraft.)

I continued, "I am experienced, I do have hours, and I have flown in worse than this." At this time I was flying in Papua New Guinea, which is renowned for difficult flying.

Once I had an engine shot out in Angola and flew over 112 nautical miles on one engine in order to keep my passengers and my FO safe. I flew that distance rather than put down at a nearby airfield, because we had been told it was suspected to be held by the rebels. I, of course, would have been taken hostage, not a pleasant experience. Two of my colleagues had been held hostage and they were both men. Women usually fared worse in a hostage situation.

So here is this short-arse upstart telling me how to fly. He was putting me down saying that if he had come to grief I most surely would, and that I should take his advice. He told the others that I 'had tickets' on myself. Talk about the pot calling the kettle black! What a fucking dick! I threw him and his crew out, offering to feed them through a propeller feet-first. He could not believe that a woman could take him apart like I did. But he didn't know that I had flown in 15 countries. He and his compatriots stood around and waited to see if I would come to grief. Being a big head, I did the most perfect crosswind landing right on the centreline. 'I showed him', I thought, but I got my comeuppance a couple of weeks later when I was teaching a student 'circuits', which are continuous take-offs and landings. I stuffed up big time and forgot to retract my flaps. Serves me right for being an arse. But it's a good lesson. If you are an old-time pilot you will smile and say 'been there done that', and if you are a new pilot it's wise to know that no matter how much experience you have, you can still make a mistake.

***

My next encounter involved a group of men who wanted to leave early for Northam, where there was a fly-in. Pilots come from all over for fly-ins—they are a lot of fun with air shows, spot landings, ribbon cutting and balloon popping. They instructed that I be there to depart them at 0700 hours, but I said no, as I already had an early start that morning to get someone else away at 0600.

As one of the men was a commercial pilot, he was perfectly capable of flying them without my help. Later that day, at 1600 hours I received a phone call from them announcing they were leaving. I said, "Okay, I will still be here as you will be in at 17:30, so appreciate you being on time."

It was agreed I would wait so the hangar could be locked up before I left for my daily walk on the beach. They finally turned up at 18.45. I expected them to come straight in but no, despite knowing I had something I wanted to do and that I had already gone well beyond the call of duty in doing their daily inspection (pre-flight) their aircraft and flight planning etc. they took their time. In the end I went out and said, "Come on fellas, I have things to do."

One twit said, "It sounds like you want a fight."

I said, "No but in theory, now that I have been here for 12 hours I have to take tomorrow off." (At the time pilots who pulled a 12-hour tour of duty had to have the next day off.)

"Would you like to explain that to Blair (the boss) for me, when the place does not open? If you want to fight, you should know that I fight like the honey badger."

"How does the honey badger fight?" asked this loud-mouthed, belligerent dick.

I replied, "They go straight for the balls."

Immediately, he replied, "But you don't have any."

I said, "No I don't, but I know where yours are located," and threw him out.

A couple of days later Blair returned and said, "My neighbour tells me you threatened to rearrange his genitalia."

"Yes," I said, "I cannot stand idiots."

***

The other two incidents were just hiccups. One gentleman had a false sense of entitlement. He was so late to his lesson that he tried to throw the student who had booked after him out of the aircraft. "I had it booked first!"

"Yes, but at 1400 hours—not 1530—there is a lesson booked after yours and you have missed out." Gross indignation!

I said that there are other aircraft but he only wanted that one. He kept trying to get the student to give up the aircraft, as 'he booked first'. I politely explained that is what we have timepieces, clocks or watches, even mobiles for, he was just trying to impress some chick by proving that he could fly an aircraft. Another one bites the dust.

The last one was my colleague, and a bully. No one bullies me so when he tried, I very quickly sorted him out and then the coward went and told on me. That's what I like, a man with balls. Bully a female but when she bites, run crying to a higher up. What a coward! I had a rocky relationship with my mother but she taught me to stand up for myself and fight back when bullies try to intimidate you. When I was three, we were on holiday and a little boy of about six pulled my hair and pushed me over. I ran crying to my mother who immediately smacked me and said, "I am teaching you to box. Anytime you get hit and cry I will hit you harder than he did." So, the next day, the little charmer came back for another go, not knowing I had been taught to box.

Heeding my mother's words, I knocked him down, but unfortunately, we were at the top of some stairs and he fell and broke his leg. As his mother came over demanding that my mother take action, she just said, "Like the action you have taken as he has punched, bitten and pulled the hair of all the other children and been an absolute brat? You sort him out, I will sort her out, but until then she is getting an ice cream." I have never let a bully get away with anything since then. I love ice cream.

So, that colleague of mine had little hope in bullying me. I was in like Flynn. On being told I wasn't to do it again, one of the students whom I had been protecting and had overheard the conversation said, "Don't berate her, just as well she sorted him out—if it had been left to my fellow student and I (they had asked not to fly with him) we would have sorted him out somewhat differently. He was lucky he just got told."

Chapter 7
This Is Your Captain Speaking

If it is a beautiful day, you know the trip will be just another flight. However, on one such beautiful day in Vanuatu, I was flying from Espirito de Santo to Port Vila. The traffic boys had put on a slightly inebriated gentleman, who liked fiddling with the rear door handle in the Twin Otter. He was causing nervousness in the other passengers, who didn't know that the door is designed so that it will not open in flight. Realising I couldn't not leave the controls and go back and talk to him, they kindly sent him to me. He was belligerent, to say the least and came on quite aggressively, stating that he was a man and would do as he wanted.

I picked up the fire axe and asked him if he wanted a new part in his hair. All this time I continued to fly the aircraft, although I had put it on the autopilot so I could turn in my seat. He looked at me holding the small axe, saw the look on my expressive face and immediately backed off saying, "No Captain, where do you want me to sit?" On disembarking, he did come up to apologise. So a beautiful day can be deceiving. There is still the thrill and excitement of other traffic on a nice day and there could be a lot of weekend warriors about so you need to keep a good look out.

Chapter 8
Preparation

The colour of the sea, the wind on the sea, and the lace pattern that forms on the top of the waves tells you in what direction the wind is coming from. The flight usually starts long before the engine actually kicks into life. In Vanuatu, we did not get daily weather reports on the main airports and nothing at all on the grass strips, so being able to read the waves was very important. It was not until we had a cyclone come through without any warning that weather reports were considered a necessity.

First-world countries do not experience these problems. The flight plan must be filed and there are restricted areas to consider in case permission is needed to fly through them. The weather forecast can show 'holding', this is weather phenomena in an area that could affect the flight and may mean you need to circle for a while. I learnt to do holding patterns around coral reefs. You simply take your compass reading on lining up on the reef and then do two-minute legs, turning 90 degrees at the end of each two minutes, with the two end turns being of one-minute duration. Works every time. Thunderstorms for instance may mean you need to circle for up to an hour and this must be allowed for by carrying extra fuel. On one occasion, I was doing a check on my young colleague who had just gained the requisite hours and had flown to my satisfaction, I had cleared him to be let loose in a twin aircraft, carrying passengers. As the time for his afternoon departure approached and the weather started to roll in, I said to him, "Would you like me to come with you? There are a few storms about."

"No, no, I will be okay, I have finally got you out of the aircraft, I want to go on my own."

"Okay, no problem."

However, just before departure his head poked around my door, "Are you busy?"

"No," I said, "would you like me to come with you?"

"Would you mind? The weather has really deteriorated."

"No worries," I said, as I grabbed my headset and headed for the aircraft.

On our return flight, we met a very large 'Charlie Bravo' (impending thunderstorm). Andy continued to head resolutely towards it. I said, "What about that thunderstorm ahead?"

He said, "It is on my track."

I said, "So what are you going to do?"

He looked so worried. I said, "Okay, pick up the mike and say 'Request'. They, being Flight Service, will say 'Go ahead' and you say 'Request to divert 10 nautical miles' or whatever you think you need east or west of track due to CB activity. They will come back with approved or an alternative depending on other traffic."

God bless his little cotton socks, he waited till we landed before he chucked me out and said, "I don't need you anymore," with the biggest grin on his face. Many pilots do their instrument ratings in a given period and chances are they fly through the whole rating without ever shooting an approach in anger, in other words, in actual weather. That word 'Request' is one of the most important they will ever learn. I tell all new instrument-rated pilots to learn 'Request'. Large aircraft these days still do the basic approaches.

***

Chapter 9
Still Learning

I often laughed at Andy, yes, I was older and he would graciously say, "You don't fly too bad for an old person."

I would say to him when we flew together, "By the time you hit that glide path you should be configured." In other words, you should be ready to land— no last-minute panic about getting flaps out and gear down. You, of course, would not have last stage of flap and to apply at last minute can cause a ballooning effect that puts you back in cloud with complete loss of visibility. Sometimes you must decide whether to go for that flap, and try to control ballooning or land with less than full flap. It is an interesting thought—no aircraft that I know of allows for operation with anything other than take-off flap, usually 10 degrees, or full flap, so to operate outside these parameters is questionable. Explaining this to Andy, he would nod, never arguing with me as he was always diplomatic.

But then after a flight test, he came in and said, "The test officer said I would have made it easier for myself if I had configured before glide path."

You also quickly learn about rate of descent. Depending on airspeed of the aircraft, you are flying a descent rate of 600-700 feet per minute and that it would put you on the three-degree glide path. Andy constantly ignored my suggestions until the test officer was in our area testing once again. He said to Andy, "Andy, 600-700 feet per minute gives you the three percent glide path." Andy would then come and tell me about this newly learnt information. I think this is great, frustrating yes, but it told me he would not take anything at face value. He gathered his information from more than one source. I might add I was still doing those same tests every year. The same ones he did.

However, I believe a new requirement has just been introduced which is LNAV & L/NAN/R/NAV which, are basically just GPS approaches which have higher minimas.

Unusual attitude recovery, for instance, has changed. An aircraft can enter an unusual attitude due to losing spatial awareness and all pilots are taught to recover the aircraft back to level flight, should this occur. The old analogue systems have a different recovery method to the new digital display. It is this that the older pilots need to be aware of. The advancements in aircraft mean that a pilot must keep up with changes in all aspects of aviation.

***

You need to check off the maintenance release for the aircraft to ensure the required work has been done and any defects cleared. You need to check if the aircraft is within hours or date in regards to services, because they are allowed a working span of one hundred hours (flight time) or twelve months before they must be serviced, depending on which criteria arises first.

On the daily inspection, we check the fuel for contamination and make sure that the aircraft is serviceable. When all this is done, we can 'commit aviation'. I always use that term because it sounds naughty. I guess that is how I look at flying, anything that gives that much pleasure and that much happiness, must indeed be naughty. Sounds like committing adultery, at least in my mind. That was always fun if he had a twelve-inch tongue and could breathe through his ears. Naughty, delicious, love it.

***

As I walk toward an aircraft, my mind is still working; if I have passengers, I must brief them on the exits, smoking, seat belts, and anything else that we consider important for that particular flight. If I am on my own or with passengers I fly from the left seat, if I am instructing, I fly from the right. Even when I am instructing, the thrill is still there because I am passing on the ability to feel as I do, that feeling of glee.

My eyes will usually do a quick flick over the aircraft; have I removed the pitot cover? The pitot tube is how we get airspeed. Total air pressure enters the tube on the aircraft and in a position of relatively undisturbed air there is a static vent which cancels out the static pressure in the total pressure, the display on the instrument is dynamic and shown as indicated airspeed.

On getting settled in the aircraft and talking to the tower, we get a start if needed and airways and taxi clearance. I usually do the checks before the passengers get on board because to have them sitting in an aircraft that is not air-conditioned in 40 degrees of heat is unpleasant and another quick check of the controls is mandatory before take-off and becoming airborne. Many pilots who have forgotten to check the controls are 'full and free' (meaning there is full movement in them) have crashed and died because they have left control locks in. These are put into an aircraft to protect them from getting damaged through extreme wind conditions. To have control surfaces flapping about uncontrollably may damage them. The control column lock would mean when it was time to rotate (lift off) because you have reached flying speed suddenly it will not respond, and at high speed with runway end approaching the possibility of death is very real. Not so bad at a large airport with made runway, a smaller aircraft may be all right but on a bush strip forget it—you are dead. The rudder, which also locks, will help correct a wing drop and spin, but if not removed then you have problems. Elevator/tail plane won't go up or down. Clear for take-off received, flight airspeed reached, gentle backpressure. Then wheels are off the ground and you are airborne; and so the adventure begins with, that joyful, excited intake of breath.

These days, I like to do ferry flights, where I can savour the feeling all by myself. Not long ago, the tower kept me high and they had asked me to keep my speed up, (conflicting traffic) then suddenly they said, "Sierra Lima Mike clear to land."

I was very close to the runway but I had lots of hours on this type of aircraft and I knew how to get it down without problems.

I simply raised the nose with power fully back, this brought the aircraft speed back into the flap extension range. I put my flaps down and it was just like I was floating; it was beautiful as the aircraft hovered as much as a fixed wing can and I came down so quietly and peacefully and quickly. I was able to taxi off the runway at the first taxiway. It was just like that.

People talk about the responsibility; I have never felt that, if I am safe, they are safe, and so I fly for my own survival. Different aircraft types call on different skills and it doesn't matter what aircraft you are flying; the challenge is still there. One day before departure to one of the Duke Islands, a small archipelago of islands off the Queensland coast which we serviced, I received a phone call from the island warning that the wind was blowing forty knots; that is quite a wind. Because of the shape and terrain of the island and the very short runway strip, a wind that strong can cause problems. Depending on the wind direction there can be a whole set of problems; if it is from the south-west you get wing drops and rotors on approach, if from the south-east you got rotors that can force you into the sea on take-off. It was rough and I needed power on approach to overcome the conditions and to avoid going off the end of the short 450-metre runway, with no reverse thrust on aircraft. Approaching with almost full power is different to a normal approach and can be elating when you land.

One day on this short runway I had brake failure, immediate response was to cut the mixture.

Mixture is the levers that control the fuel/air ratio to the engine. With no fuel, no power, the aircraft comes to a stop. Initially it is a shock when something like brake failure happens, that shock can cause a delay in action and could have been more serious, it also hampers a short-field take-off. Short-field take-offs are achieved using take-off flap full power and stand on the brakes. When the aircraft is shaking itself to bits, release brakes and you are airborne shortly after.

I love the sheer excitement and exhilaration as you face each day with a new set of problems. Mountains that look huge at ground level flatten out before your eyes as you approach them. Rivers that look like raging torrents or muddy flows suddenly take on a whole new appearance; like a snake winding through the landscape when seen from altitude.

Different countries have different landscapes and your horizons broaden. I was flying with a colleague one day and we were getting close to sunset. But we were still going to be on the ground before it actually set. He asked me to fake a sunset by using the cloud in conjunction with the sun to make it look like a sunset, and by manoeuvring the aircraft we created an illusion of a sunset. It was amazing! Sunset made to order. When flying in Sweden, the Northern Lights dancing around the aircraft wings creates an amazing spectacle. It doesn't matter how long I live; I shall always have those special memories.

I cannot remember a flight where I haven't learnt something and often say I shall give up the day I stop learning. Hopefully you learn from your mistakes. This is what I say to students who come in disheartened because they have been disappointed by their performance that day. "Hey, when I had your hours, I did this. Now, how stupid is that?" This achieves two things: they learn how to operate the equipment and they realise that the instructor they have held in awe is capable of making errors and mistakes and not all mistakes have a fatal outcome. The ability to laugh at oneself is so important. I read in an aviation magazine that on any flight there are 27 errors. It can be a wrong call back to tower or from tower, you could set the 'QNH' wrong (QNH is a code that was made when Morse code was a primary source of communication. As Morse code became less used, many of the codes fell into disuse, however, some codes in aviation are still used.) You could forget to let the passengers out (seat belts) and have to be reminded by the cabin crew. None of this is fatal. Yes, it could lead to a chain of events that causes serious problems, but that is why we have a checklist. If interrupted by a call from tower, most crew have a memory cue to remind them. All the crew I have operated with do; some companies put in place a particular memory recall.

***

Chapter 10
Easy Navigation These Days

No one gets lost these days, but that's only because of sat-nav or GPS. Many years ago, one pilot got lost and dropped his passengers off at a dirt strip while he looked around. Unfortunately he then lost the strip, and it was a mad search to find his passengers again before they succumbed to the heat of the outback. GPS has saved the day. This sort of incident no longer happens.

I find it interesting that Australia's safety record is no better than Papua New Guinea's, which is where some of the most dangerous flying in the world takes place. Rock-lined clouds kill so many. The difference is that in PNG, commercial pilots die, whereas in Australia it's private pilots, or those flying light home-built aircraft. These days, I think the commercial pilot is safer, as with the pilot shortage they can be pickier about who they work for, and don't have to accept shonky operators.

I would like to say the Civil Aviation Safety Authority (CASA) plays a part in improving safety outcomes, but in my experience the men and women they send out into the field have been quite ineffectual. Many don't know the rules. They send people out to lecture pilots on new rules, but their knowledge is usually lacking. I had two men come to the last airport I worked at, where airport management were nothing but a bunch of bullies. The representatives of CASA came and spouted forth such garbage. One said, Australia was going to follow the USA and become compliant with International Civil Aviation Organisation (ICAO) regulations. When I pointed out that the USA is not ICAO compliant, they argued until I pointed out discrepancies. As an agency of the United Nations, ICAO's rules were formed just after the Second World War and while the United States is a member, it does not comply with their regulations.

These poor bastards were being sent out to deal with people of my experience, who had flown in so many countries and knew so many regulations. To be presented with the wrong information said nothing good about the Australian regulator. These poor bastards hated me, but as I have said before, I have trouble with inefficiency and stupidity.

***

While working in Port Hedland—a very male-dominated mining town, I engaged in a different sort of flying. I learnt to fly navigating by what shouldn't be there. There was no GPS back then, so we flew a track for the estimated time that we had worked out in our flight plan, allowing for wind—head wind, tailwind and across track (drift), we should arrive over the target destination. However, map reading is a talent. In populated areas, there are towns, railway tracks, major roads and highways. By looking at where a railway track crosses a road, you can work out what town you're looking down at.

Navigating by what shouldn't be there, meant now I was looking for not only natural geographic features, but man-made features like a dirt track, old shed or homestead, which were few and far between. I saw a lot of rivers devoid of water. Port Hedland sits between two weather systems or areas known for rain. Further north, you have the weather that is connected to the Inter Tropical Convergence Zone, known to pilots as the ITCZ. This brings the tropical rains and monsoon to Northern Australia, also the weather that comes up from the Southern Ocean has rain. But Port Hedland itself is dry. With this new environment came new challenges, and new people. They call themselves 'Norwesters' and some of them are more like Crocodile Dundee than any people I have met before or after. Swung from the hip, chest puffed out, and corks on the hat. Of course, the most butch of all of them asked me out. We had been dating for a while when my boss asked if I could go out to an aboriginal community to pick up a young mother who was about to give birth. The Royal Flying Doctor Service (RFDS) was unable to make the trip as the landing strips tend to break up with their larger aircraft at that time of year. I agreed to do it but recalled that I had a date scheduled with the macho man that evening, and needed to let him know I could no longer make it. I knocked loudly on his door and yelled his name, but didn't get an answer. I knew he was home because his car was in the drive and no one walks anywhere in Hedland, it's just too hot.

You could live 100 yards from the local shopping centre but you never walked, as nearly every day was over 40 degrees Centigrade, and it only rained two days every five years, when the young children would run in to tell Mum the sky was crying.

I knocked again with no reply, so in the end I reached my hand under the doormat for the spare key and let myself in to write a note. Imagine my surprise to find 'my man' struggling to divest himself of a bra and suspender belt. Stunned I blurted out, "I can't go to dinner tonight…or ever again!" and ran for my car to go back to the airport.

Once the aircraft was ready, we departed, and working together with the RFDS crew to file flight plans, while the engineer removed seats and set up points to secure the stretcher and a seat for the nurse. The community we were visiting was called Punmu and it was out past Telfer, a very remote mining town. Mining towns have clinics to assist injured miners, however with the RFDS' record of two hours from first notification to providing assistance, the clinics remain basic. Telfer is such a large mining community that it had a navigation aid, and after reaching there, it was only about half an hour further on. We picked up the expectant mother and transported her to Port Hedland without incident. We arrived, without me having to update the flight log with an extra soul on board.

Another first in this area for me was landing by bonfire, stations (ranches or large farms) use jam tins half-filled with kerosene, which they set alight to mark the runway. The positioning of a car with its lights can indicate wind direction, but there was none of this available when I broke down. I had been out to a mine called Moomba to drop off personnel. On departure, the aircraft would not start. An aeronautical engineer from my company was dispatched, hitching a ride with another company. Once he had fixed the problem, we made our way back to base. The aircraft was an Apache (PA23)—one of the Piper range, it was a four-seat twin. As we headed back into Port Hedland the Flight Service called me up to say they had an emergency. The community health nurses, whom we called the 'dick and fanny doctors' because they treat (pregnancy and sexually transmitted disease cases—the most common problems in the local communities), had spent the day at a particular community where their aircraft had broken down. They were worried as to whether they would be safe overnight, so I was asked to divert into the community. It was fairly early in my time in the area, and I asked the Flight Service how many nurses there were. "Three," came the reply.

I said, "I've only got room for two."

"Throw your engineer out, you can get him tomorrow," came the answer. I requested coordinates.

"Fly to the De Grey River. When you get there turn right and follow the river. When they hear you, they will light fires."

The De Grey has water in it, probably once every five years—dry and arid is the word. But I found the De Grey and turned right, when up ahead all of a sudden, I saw fire. Big bonfires lit up the night sky. I landed, threw out the engineer and got the girls home safely to Port Hedland.

Another time, I was asked to pick up a 13-year old girl, as she was pregnant and due to her lack of record keeping, no one was sure if she was 32 weeks or 36 weeks into her pregnancy. While being tested and examined it was discovered that she had won the trifecta. She had gonorrhoea, chlamydia and syphilis. Unfortunately, no one was surprised, as we hardened pilots and medical staff had seen it all before. Of course, at 13 years old, the girl's father or brothers were more than likely the father of the child.

Chapter 11
Cessnock

I enjoyed working in the outback; the flying was different, and people were different. They were openhearted and generous. My macho man came by a few days later to explain and to thank me for not telling anyone about him. He was not gay; he was a transvestite and they like dressing up for a variety of reasons. However, back then he would have been thought to be 'queer'. In a town like Port Hedland 'poofter-bashing' still took place in 1986. 'Poofter' in the Australian vernacular means homosexual. It seems strange now to think that back then people died for their sexual preferences. I guess they still do when you read the news and see that some countries still allow this to happen. But this was Australia and this town had one of the largest AIDS clinics in Australia at that time, as there was only one woman for every five men. There was much homosexual activity, it was just not acknowledged or openly accepted. And quite often, those that practiced such activities would be first in line to deliver the bashing should others be discovered in this sort of relationship.

On returning to Melbourne, I applied and was successful for a CFI position in Cessnock, run by a gentleman who really did have both hands on his dick moving furiously. It was run as a paramilitary operation. I have never believed in paramilitary operations; I find it just an excuse for some knob to pretend he is important.

It might impress some parents but on the whole, it is a complete fail. You're either in the military or a civilian—not both. Of course, wearing uniform is a good thing, it gets the students thinking about presentation. How would you feel if you saw your pilot turning up in shorts or sweats? To tell the truth, he or she wouldn't fly any differently, they would do everything the same, making the same decisions. Pilots are trained to the highest degree of professionalism. They can be either military or civilian, it doesn't matter; the uniform commands respect. So, while in training it doesn't do any harm for the students to be in uniform, that is where the advantage stops. These schools are nothing more than sausage machines and the students really learn to fly when they get out in the real world, where they are dealing with the shonky operators, where they have to learn to say "no." So here I was working at this paramilitary school where one of the greatest twits I have ever met was the CEO. Anytime a student had to go to his office to talk to him about a problem with their training, they would need to see this man who had on his wall a picture of a Dornier 328. When the student had finished trying to talk to him, he would point to the Dornier and say, "When you can fly that, you can talk to me, till then you are dismissed."

I resigned once again, as already stated, stupidity and inefficiency doesn't sit well with me.

***

While in this salubrious town, located in the wine growing area of the Hunter Valley, I met a man who decided I was just what he wanted. I was not interested, there was something in his eyes that was hard and unflinching. Turns out he was an underground mine manager and they have to be tough. But he didn't leave it behind when he left work. So I continued to say no. He flooded the office with flowers, chocolates, wine. His persistence paid off and when we went to dinner he was out to impress. As we walked into the restaurant, he called the maître de by name, the man had done his homework.

"Table for two please, Daryl."

We were shown to a secluded little corner and seated. The wine waiter came and asked if we would like wine. I don't really drink but I said okay. I had recognised signs of drink in him and thought 'what the hell—he will drink it anyway'. So off tottered the sommelier to find a bottle of wine and came back with it displayed along his arm, pointing out the name, type, date and relevant details to a connoisseur of wine (of which I was not). The sommelier uncorked the bottle and went to pour some wine into my date's glass when he shoved his hand across the top of the glass saying, "NAH, YUH SERVE THE LADY FIRST."

Being the lady that I am, I fell out of my chair laughing. All that effort for nothing, except one date rolling on the floor laughing. I still smile when I think of that.

Chapter 12
Outback

So off I went to Darwin for a new job that only lasted four days before I got sacked. I had a disagreement with the boss because I didn't find his airplanes safe to fly due to poor maintenance. Un-airworthy, we call that in aviation. As I walked around the airport looking for a new position, a fantastic man employed me. He was short, fat and full of bluster but had a very kind heart. He asked how I had come to be in Darwin and I told him the story of this other operator.

He decided to give me a chance. Most of the men he had working for him were anti-female pilots, or so he thought. In truth, these guys gave me lots of encouragement. The boss worked on the idea that if he could cause dissension, he had the advantage. I have the ability to get people to unite as a team, so I worked well with the guys.

That being said, I must admit I also have an abrasive side to my nature and I am quick with repartee. I don't think he had ever had anyone work for him before who could come back with a quick reply. This short man could fly, boy could he fly. He had been in the Olympics representing Australia in boxing and fencing. I am not sure if he ever won medals, but he was quite the sportsman in his younger years. As well as owning the company, he owned a Pitts Special aerobatic plane, which he flew like he was part of the machine, he was brilliant in the air. One day, he was giving me a hard time about something and said, "You do realise I am a chauvinist and your worst nightmare."

I just laughed and said, "No, you're not; you are just an arsehole as you treat the male pilots as badly as you treat me." He just looked, never said anything, but I, who always have had a ready reply plus a very blue sense of humour, gave as good as I got. The next day, he was helping load the aircraft, as part of the job was getting supplies to the many different indigenous communities that inhabit this northern part of Australia. He was sitting on the floor of the aircraft using his feet to kick this '2 x 4' package into a space of about '2 x 2'.

I grinned and said, "Ever thought of using KY Jelly?" The poor man just went extremely red in the face with embarrassment. I am deliberately not using his name as he still has family living in the Northern Territory.

I remember him crying when he spoke about Cyclone Tracy, which wiped out Darwin in the Christmas of 1974. He recalled walking around with a pistol on his hip as looters were to be shot on sight. Different laws in those days, no do-gooders making excuses. He was helping the police and emergency services and part of that job was looking for bodies and body parts, trying to match arms and legs to a torso. As he told this story, the tears coursed down his face. The official death toll of Cyclone Tracy was 71, but he maintained that a boat had gone out for a cruise and dinner around the harbour when the cyclone hit. According to him there were 87 on board and all lives were lost. This was never reported as no bodies were found. Crocodiles and sharks probably had a good feed that day. The rest of Australia had no knowledge of this disaster until well after it actually happened and not even the residents of Darwin had ever seen a storm of such ferocity. In its approach everyone had taken refuge, a cyclone has two sides and the eye in the middle. Those days, not as much was known about cyclones, and to make matters worse, it was a very slow-moving cyclone. Those are the worst type because they move so slowly, it seems like they last forever and the damage is more intense. So many people were killed during Tracy because it was so slow moving and long lasting that people thought it was all over when the eye of the cyclone arrived and the winds died. People left their homes and places of safety to replenish stocks of beer and food when along came the second side. It was mainly these people who were taken by surprise and died because of flying debris, cars being blown off causeways and falling trees. It was such a mammoth destruction that the town was flattened. This man came through all of this and was still operating and fighting the good fight. When a cyclone is approaching the pilots are usually called in and told to fly the aircraft to another safe location.

***

He was a greater innovator; importing two new types of aircraft to Australia, a Beechcraft Baron with long-range tanks and an Italian aircraft—a Partenavia. Both new to the conditions of the Australian bush, he had studied the pros and cons of the purchases and both aircraft types operated and are still operating in Australia. He was a clever, thinking man who, with his experience, lived on a short fuse.

One day, two Civil Aviation Authority (CAA) later to become the Civil Aviation Safety Authority (CASA) inspectors arrived on his premises and started to throw their weight about unnecessarily, just bullying, saying he was not compliant according to them. They threatened him, so he decked them and threw them out. He was later taken to court for that one. Bless his little cotton socks; I know exactly how he felt. Some people can't handle authority and many of the CASA inspectors think they are better than you, when in reality they are often failed operators, some questionable in my opinion. The other inspectors are often ex-air force and have never had to pay for a flying lesson in their life.

But here, under his tutelage I learnt what aviation is really about. It was here I really learnt to fly, during the monsoon season, there was much to learn. Here in Darwin, there is a thunderstorm that has its own name as it forms every day during the wet season at the same time, runs its little route and drops its load of heavy rain over Snake Bay. It is called HECTA/HECTOR and its stands for Heat Equatorial Convergence Trough. It is one of the most predictable thunderstorms in the world. It is also one of the tallest thunderstorms, reaching to the tropopause. The tropopause has three heights. Lowest at the poles where the air is denser, the tropopause at the Equator is much higher. The tropopause ranges between 23000' at the poles to 65000' at the equator. One job I had was to take three meteorologists from overseas to the Tiwi Islands. Melville and Bathurst Islands are the two most affected by this phenomenon. These meteorologists would make camp for three months at the airport and study the thunderstorm.

On another trip my boss sent me to Katherine with the Beechcraft Baron where I was to help an Aboriginal Affairs Officer to transport three local tribesmen to a settlement called 'Bulman'. They told me it is impossible for a native Australian to get lost in his own land. This means his tribal land, not the whole of Australia, or lands that are not considered their tribal land. In their own tribal land, you cannot fault their navigation. These would be the people you would want on board to give you a hand with navigation when marking the sacred sites on their land. What to you or me is just a bunch of rocks, to them it has significance, as one of the rocks will signify water, another distance, direction and anything else that was needed to support life. Remember that the aborigines were nomadic and traversed the great continent of Australia in this way for at the last estimate, 65,000 years. They are brilliant trackers as their ability to read the ground kept them fed. They were hunter-gatherers and this is one of the reasons when Captain Cook arrived on our shores, he declared Australia 'Terra Nullis', which means vacant land. The tribesmen he did meet, had no communities and roamed, gathering their tucker as they went along. They appeared to have no laws, no punishment and no penalties, where in fact they did have laws and punishments. Back then, if you had committed a crime in their eyes you could be sentenced to a spearing. Spearing still takes place today, but back then it was a death sentence. Because they speared you in the leg it was basically a sentence of starvation as you could no longer run to catch game or hunt as you were lame. Today however, when a spearing takes place, they call up the Royal Flying Doctor Service and the victim is taken to hospital where he/she makes a full recovery and returns to their community healed. There was one punishment reserved for only the most serious of crimes, I would think probably of a sexual nature or continuous crimes against the tribe. To stop the perpetrator producing offspring who might well follow in his ways, they use to cauterise the penis so he could not ejaculate normally through the end of the penis. They somehow make an incision in the underside of the penis so when he had sex his sperm falls on the ground so to speak and did not enter the women's vagina. These days, the indigenous people are confined to communities and no longer live in a nomadic fashion. So when I arrived in Katherine, I had to take the Aboriginal Affairs officer plus the three men to Bulman. They came to mark the sacred sites of the area under consideration for mining. I arrived early, as I still do to this day. Time came and went, so I rang my boss and told him no one had shown up. "WAIT," was his command and eventually after many hours three men arrived instead of four. The excuse was that the men had come in from their communities and many communities are dry, so alcohol is not permitted. The elders of the tribe usually make this rule, as it is normally the younger members who like the alcohol. So in town, where alcohol was available, it was a bit too much of a temptation for these gentlemen, who had spent the night getting drunk and fighting. The gentleman from Aboriginal Affairs had spent a lot of time bailing them out, however the third gentleman was still incarcerated as he had been particularly violent and was not given bail. The more sober of the two was put in the front with me to assist with navigation. He was wearing a pair of stubby shorts, which had very short legs and as he sat on the front seat all his genitalia were displayed. He had a little dilly bag with Kentucky Fried Chicken and proceeded to chew on a chicken leg.

With the sight and smell of food, the other man in the back started to throw up and then went to sleep as he was feeling so unwell. The man from Aboriginal Affairs leant forward saying, "It will settle," when he noticed my 'co-pilot' was displaying more of himself than normal. I have never seen anyone get so embarrassed, but he was determined to press on. This decision was costing the Australian taxpayer lots of dollars. Mineral rights are owned by the Crown, the landowner has no rights over their land, although thirty percent of land that is affected by mining is owned by the Aborigine. They were losing use of their land and sacred sites were being damaged with no benefit to them. Over the years, this flight was one of the earliest, recognising their right of land ownership was about defining sites that have importance to them. These days, the communities receive royalties from the appropriate authorities to help improve their way of life. But unfortunately, they will never resume their nomadic way of life as civilisation encroaches further into the outback.

Because of the difficulty navigating this terrain, I often had to change maps; remember this was all before GPS, this was just map reading in featureless ground. We also used military maps, topographical maps and road maps. As we were heading for Bulman, the man from Aboriginal Affairs noticed I was changing my maps so many times and told me to listen to the tribesman for navigation as you can't get lost when they are in their tribal grounds. Well it turned out Mr Genitalia wasn't in his tribal lands and his 'oba there' was way off because we ended up at a place called Mt Tin. I had noticed the discrepancy, so I turned left and diverted to the 'correct' Bulman, disregarding the guidance from the right seat. On arrival at Bulman we landed to take a break as the journey had taken twice as long thanks to my hungover navigator. After landing the gentleman in the back was suddenly recovered, feeling fine as always happens when that natural movement of aircraft is removed. It was actually a lovely smooth flight that day but not for someone suffering a hangover from the night before. We had a small break before taking off again to work out the sacred sites from the air. This time the man from Aboriginal Affairs had decided to sit in the front and put the two tribesmen in the back as it had become clear to him that my 'navigator' was not in his tribal grounds and had managed to con his way into the trip in order to receive the pay, while knowing absolutely nothing about this land.

While we had every intention of fulfilling the objective of marking the sacred sites, it quickly became apparent that it was entirely a waste of taxpayers' money. As the gentleman in the back started to become sick again Mr Genitalia wasn't much help either, as he was just munching on another chicken leg. The boss from Aboriginal Affairs said, "I give up, let's call it a day, and take us back to Katherine." Having changed direction and maps so many times that day, I realised, I had no idea where the fuck I was, as none of the maps really related to one another. I guess I must have a homing pigeon in my head, as by intuition I decided to fly heading 210 degrees until I could pick up the Stuart Highway and from there decide whether to turn left or right to Katherine. After approximately an hour, I turned on the VOR navigation aid that was located at Katherine airport. As it flickered to life, I started to rotate the Central Deviation Indicator (CDI) and it settled on the 210 radial! I still laugh when I think how professional it must have looked, but in reality, it was just a bloody fluke. That natural sense of direction I have in my head has got me out of trouble more times than I care to remember.

My boss wanted to take me off line flying (flying line is charter work and no instructing), as his CFI had just been accepted by one of Australia's major airlines and he wanted me to replace him. I was enjoying line flying too much and said no. I didn't want to work with the junior instructor, Ryan who was a brown nose. Ryan crawled to anyone who he thought could help him on his way to the top. A real slimy bastard. I said, "No, I don't wish to work with Ryan, he is a brown nose."

The boss roared at me, "How dare you say he sniffs my arse, apologise or you're fired!"

I immediately said sorry. As the smile spread across his face thinking he had won, I said, "He doesn't sniff your arse, he licks it! He doesn't have a brown nose; he has a brown tongue!" My boss lost it at that stage and physically threw me out. He told me to never darken his door again. The chief pilot rang me that night to tell me what I was doing the next day.

I said: "Haven't you heard? I got the sack."

The chief pilot told me, "Don't worry about that, all of us have been sacked four or five times; just turn up."

I said, "No thanks, you only sack me once and I stay sacked." As I look back, I fully endorse my boss' decision. There are few people I respect as much as I respected this man and am pleased to report there is a street named after him at Darwin Airport. He did sack me but I deserved it.

In Darwin, the flying was interesting as you basically only held an instrument rating to avoid thunderstorms. When talking to Flight Service you would quite often be told that there were thunderstorms or Charlie Bravos (CB) between Radial 230 to Radial 360 or whatever area the storms where in that day. One day I was standing on my veranda looking at the CB and you could literally see it growing, gaining new formations as it built. They truly are spectacular.

***

Some of the most interesting people I have met, have been due to the flying I have done in the Australian outback. The Australians that live in these remote areas are the most practical and resourceful individuals I have met.

One pilot told of how on landing at a remote dirt strip on her station with her single-engine Cessna 172, she ended up with a flat tyre. She was so used to just taking off and going out to check bores and windmills on her property that she had not informed anyone of her intended destination. She was eight months pregnant and apart from the usual first aid kit, which always contains water, she was on her own. (These days a pilot's medical certificate is immediately suspended with pregnancy in the UK). As the terrain she had flown over was inhospitable and extremely rocky, it would have taken a minimum of 24 hours to reach by car. What a lot of people don't know is that under all that terrain is a vast plateau of artesian water. Here she was, stuck without any means of contacting anyone. There was no way for her to jack the aircraft up, however, she was a typical country Australian who had grown up improvising. What I'm trying to say is that you shouldn't judge a book by its cover. This lady was a reasonably petite, glamorous woman on a night out. But equally so she was an independent, resourceful woman when the need arose. She lifted the damaged wheel off the ground by applying weight to the tail of the Cessna. Pilots normally do this so the nose comes off the ground and you can swing the aircraft easily in any direction. She had built a small mound by using rocks and then she swung the nose-wheel bracket so that it rested on the mound of rocks. Now all she had to do according to her was to get as much dry grass as she could and pack the now deflated nose wheel with dried scrub and grass. Yes it was hard work as she forced the grass into the tyre, with heat and pregnancy not making the job any easier. She stuffed as much as she could of this mixture of dried scrub leaves and grass in the wheel until it was pretty solid again. She used a selection of flap and with a short-field take-off technique she was off the ground quickly. It wasn't a perfect landing when she got home, she landed nose high and when the aircraft had run out of forward energy, she lowered the nose to the packed earth that made their home strip. After her safe arrival, she said, "I could murder a cup of tea now." To those of us she was talking to, we understood perfectly. It is about survival—staying alive in the harshest of conditions, knowing where to look for water, how to make water.

In Australia, as in the Sahara, there is water, it is not as deep as in the Sahara but having lived in both places I know there is water there. I was at a mining camp in the Sahara and it had the purest water I have ever tasted deep from beneath the earth. The mining staff had sunk a bore down 500 feet and the water was clear and pure. Unfortunately, in Australia some of our artesian water is undrinkable, but can be used for washing, cleaning or watering the garden. Many stations in Australia, like Victoria River Downs for example, are larger than some small countries. At one stage, Victoria River Downs was the world's largest pastoral property when it was first settled in 1855, however, a large tract of it was subsequently sold off. It once had an area of 41,000 square kilometres but is now less than half that size. So you can find gardens, grass, flowers and vegetables, all freshly grown in the Australian outback due to this artesian water. When they need meat, they will have a 'kill'.

So the Australians that inhabit this part of the country have been responsible for much of my attitude. Down and out? You stop feeling sorry for yourself, get off your arse and work it out.

Remember there are no victims, only volunteers. People treat you the way you allow them to treat you. Give me the people of these remote areas any time; they are all down to earth—none of the bullshit about keeping up with the Jones, like you find in the cities. They are about survival, cutting to the chase. It is through being with, and learning from these people, that I have learnt to survive.

***

Two such characters are my friend Lois and her partner Bill. I was working at an aboriginal community in Far North West Queensland and I had knocked off for the day and was cooking tea at home when the phone rang. It was Lois. Bill, was the Warden at Wathanine, an aboriginal prison farm approximately 20 nautical miles (NM) south from Aurukun—an aboriginal community. Lois said, "You have to come down here and pick up a prisoner." I cannot mention this prisoner's name as there are still family members alive and aboriginal beliefs forbid mentioning a dead person's name. I do not know if he has died but out of respect and in case he has, he shall remain nameless.

So I said, "Do tell."

Lois immediately explained he has been bitten on the dick by a dead snake. Lois unfortunately had a reputation as a practical joker, so I hung up.

Immediately, the phone rang again and Lois said, "Get down here, I am serious. You have to take him to Weipa, the ambulance will meet you at the airport."

So, off I went and arrived to find the prisoner standing with one hand over his genitalia and the other hand holding the dead snake in a plastic bag. As we got him into the aircraft and the seat belt done up, I asked Lois "HOW?!" It seems Bill had been out earlier in the day and came across the snake, back then you could kill a snake whereas nowadays they are protected. I believe it was a brown snake, a very nasty reptile to get bitten by. You die quickly unless aid is available or you know how to react while awaiting the RFDS. Bill had hung it over the fence. In Australia the aboriginals are allowed guns on the prison farms, so they can hunt for bush tucker. There is no danger of them escaping, as the rivers are filled with saltwater crocodiles—another animal not really friendly to humans—surrounded the little island they were on. The aborigines prefer to eat bush-tucker, which consists of lizards, turkeys, goannas, in fact anything that moves, with a preference for either wallabies or baby kangaroos, known as joeys.

They found the dead snake hanging over the fence. I have seen aborigines cut the fangs out of a live snake just for fun. They are not afraid of snakes, so naturally they started playing with it, prising its mouth open and gleefully putting the fangs over fingers, ears and different parts of the body. One man decided it would be funny to pretend a snake was biting his private parts, and after some tomfoolery somehow the fangs had penetrated his penis. When Lois, who is a natural comic told the story, I grinned and said, "Well, it looks like he is going to die; they won't find anyone to suck the poison out." While the situation was reasonably serious, the snake was already dead and the likelihood of the venom still having the same dangers seemed remote. We took the snake with us in the plastic bag so it could be identified for the antivenin. Approximately two weeks later I was back in Weipa to pick this prisoner up and transfer him back to the prison. I should mention the prison farm is like natural life for the Aborigine— it is the same as their community, without family, of course. It also keeps them away from alcohol, as that is usually the reason most end up in prison in the first place.

***

Chapter 13
Porno

I decided not to talk about family, but I remembered this little gem, which still causes me to laugh. I hope it does make you have a giggle, too. My mother had a neighbour called David who always wore a silly toupee. He was a good-looking man but he was bald. He was living with a black American girl named Mary, who was a happy, intelligent woman and cared so deeply for David it made your heart sing. Mary was and still is a lovely woman. Since my father died, these truly beautiful people helped my mother with all sorts of jobs and when I wasn't around, they did anything she asked to help. Mary quite often called in just to check on mother and always gave her a little gift. They were such generous lovely beings. David has since died and Mary has become a doctor.

While my father was still alive, my parents had been asked to collect David's mail while they were away on holidays. Every day my father got the mail from the mailbox. One day a brown paper package arrived, supposedly with the wrapping paper torn.

On closer examination it was revealed that there were X-rated videos in the package. This gave my mother the opportunity to say, "Oh! He is a pervert."

Sometime later when I was visiting my parents, my mother said David was a dirty, disgusting pervert. I immediately said, "How do you know?"

She regaled me with the story of the torn wrapping.

I said, "Well, that is surely his affair. What has it got to do with you? To know that those videos were disgusting and filthy you would have had to watch them. How do you know they were filthy and disgusting?"

"Oh, your father and I did watch them."

"What! All three?" I asked.

"Yes, and those women, what sluts! They let the men put it in any orifice!"

By this time I was really enjoying myself. Here was this woman, who at that time must have been seventy-eight and my father would have been eighty-one, watching porno movies!

I said, "You know Mum, that's what choice is about. You chose to violate this man's privacy by reading his mail and then you then call him names when you are no better! You have watched the same perverted movies. Being an adult is the right to exercise your rights and switch it off. If it offends you, why did you watch it?"

"Oh, well, I couldn't have called him a pervert unless I had seen and judged it for myself."

This sort of answer, she truly believes to be right. According to her, the right to infringe on someone else's privacy is her right alone. And no, she is not a pervert, a charge from me she vehemently denied. She had done nothing wrong and to this day does not see her behaviour as lacking in propriety, let alone the rules and regulations of the Royal Mail that exist to protect people's privacy. I still giggle when I think of my mother and father watching porn. Poor Dad, he was such a proper man and she was such a harridan.

***

Chapter 14
Change

The accident I was involved in that caused my thinking to change, was extremely serious and I still have problems associated with it. But these problems didn't manifest until later—much later. At that time I was just happy to have survived intact. I still worked, in other words, I could walk and talk in a muffled way as my jaws were wired together. I also had full mental process. It is this process that pulls you up short and makes you realise that this is not a dress rehearsal. This is your life and watching it pass without at least trying to fulfil your dreams is stupid. I once had a man say to me that you should always aim for the stars and if you have to land on a nearby moon, then at least you tried. I had no intention of failing. I was no longer going to be a pleaser. Yes sir, no sir, three bags full sir. Get off your arse and get it yourself! I was different. I decided to follow my dreams; I worked harder than ever and sent my kids to private schools. I wanted to give them every chance in life and for myself I decided to take flying lessons. That dream was still there. So I went and took my first flight, which was a 30-minute flight. A Trial Introductory Flight (TIF) in a Piper Cherokee and I fell in love. I have always felt that flying is a disease and if caught, incurable. I have already explained that thrill.

I still ran a business, a home, took my children to sporting events, basketball and horse riding. Two nights a week, I also went to class for the private pilot aviation subjects: basic aeronautical knowledge, flight planning, air law, aerodynamics, principles of flight and navigation.

***

I should never have held a license. You can't get your license without having a medical certificate. That accident caused severe head injuries. People who have had head injuries do not get to hold a medical certificate until having had many expensive tests and investigations. However, when I had the medical examination for my initial medical certificate, I didn't know that. The examining doctor asked lots of questions but in the whole examination he never once asked if I had suffered a head injury, and so I never told him I had indeed been seriously hurt in the past. At my next medical, two years later he did ask the question; he asked if I had a head injury in the last 12 months. By now it was four years since the accident, I had been thrown out of a car that was doing 80 miles an hour, as my ex-husband lost control and my door, plus the stanchion which the seat belt

48

was secured to, was ripped away. As the car rolled, I was thrown out, breaking quite a lot of my body. But the most serious injury broke the floor of my eyes and I now suffer from glaucoma and teeth problems as many of my teeth were damaged in this accident. I was scared, but I healed quickly. The scars had become unnoticeable as I have an animated face that when I speak of flying becomes more so. The scars, while still there, are also more visible as I age. Had I been asked if I have ever had a head injury, I would have been my usual self and answered honestly, but I wasn't asked. Nor did I know that a head injury precluded holding a license. I got my medical certificate and was set to change my life. Brilliant. I made new friends, my outlook changed and I was in love, a true love that has lasted forever.

***

My change of attitude was a big difference. Any previous request was answered with, "Yes, how high do you want me to jump?" I might have grumbled, but I jumped.

Now, I said, "No." No more weekend drives. I went flying. I even learnt to fly helicopters at a later date! What a blast! I still remembered my helicopter theory after having got into an argument the other week about principles of flight and aerodynamics on a reported helicopter accident. I was proven right in the subsequent investigation. Once learnt, you do not forget. I shall probably go in to the crematorium thinking of my 'start procedure checklist'. I always think flying a helicopter is a bit like making love in a hammock: everything is moving at once. When I learnt to fly helicopters they were not as easy to fly as today, where things are more automatic with the governor controlling the RPM as you raise the cyclic. I had too many fixed wing hours by the time I was learning helicopters and did not transition well, but it is still my favourite sort of flying. The exhilaration is MAGIC!

***

Chapter 15
Flying

I became hooked, in love with the joy of flying and the feeling of accomplishment. I went on to do a night license, which I had entered a competition for and it was partly paid for by the Australian Women Pilots' Association. I still hadn't decided to become a professional at this time. It seems that once you have acquired a license your flying comes to a full stop. Going down for a bit of a run, no thrill no challenge, so I took up aerobatics and became proficient at negative work. Doing negative work means pulling negative G. G-Force is the force of gravity. I would go high and start with a negative spin, changing it to a positive spin on the way down, bloody good fun but stressful on the body. I, at one stage, had a range of G-force that went from 3 negative G to 6 positive G, which is quite a good range for someone who was in their early forties. Once I had my instructors rating, I did teach aerobatics as it was good fun. I loved it. I was up practicing with the man who had taught me the advanced aerobatics when we had a spin go wrong. One in every 1000 spins goes wrong. We had started high and he told me to 'recover' and as the aircraft didn't respond, he yelled again 'RECOVER' but it wouldn't, so we tried together, but still no response. Then as we passed 3000 feet, we both yelled, "Hands and feet off!" It recovered at 1800 feet on its own. I still tell students when you have tried all you know and you're in trouble, take your hands and feet off and let it fly itself. Aircraft are meant to fly; it is the idiot behind the joystick or control column that stops it flying. What made me give up aerobatics? One flight, I went from pulling negative G to pulling positive G and I swear I felt my brain slosh around in my skull like jelly. That scared me and I gave up extreme aerobatics that day.

I will also admit that at this stage my marriage was in trouble and I could go and throw the aircraft around the sky and forget all my angst. You need to be very fit to do extreme acrobatics, at the time I was participating in this sport I was extremely fit. I was swimming at a local pool during my lunch break and I started swimming a mile a day. It didn't matter where I went, I always kept the swimming up—a lot cheaper than hiring an aircraft to throw around the sky. When I first went to the UK the CAA there picked up a strange wave in my heart. I can't explain it better than that, it was just an anomaly and it seems that I had been born with it. Because they the doctors could prove I was born with it there was no problem, but as explained to me, if it had happened during my lifetime then I would not have been able to hold a license. The stress of it all saw me at the pool and by now I was swimming two kilometres. Because of all this exercise my heart rate is extremely slow. But I was fit and entered the London Fun Run in 1989, completing 10 kilometres so not a marathon, but I still remember running over Tower Bridge.

***

Chapter 16
Helicopters

While I was learning helicopters, I had gone solo and was trying to build some solo hours. There had been a lot of banter with one of the men working as a chopper pilot. He was not an instructor, but he was there most of the time. They check transmission lines and do rescue work, joy flights, charters—the same as any other commercial pilot, doing what they can to build hours. This gentleman had been flirting with me for some time and as I ventured out to go solo, he came to talk. I was carrying out a pre-flight inspection when he came up and said, "Let's make a bet."

"Oh yes," said I, "on what and how much?"

"No money involved; the bet is that I can make you lose your concentration."

I laughed and said, "No way, I will be up there, you cannot make me lose my concentration in the air."

"Well, come on, put your money where your mouth is," said Mr Smarty Pants.

How wrong I was. I just got the helicopter into the hover when he came into my peripheral vision and dropped his pants and brown eyed me. Yes, the helicopter wavered as I giggled, while he jumped up and down elated. He had won. The bet was if I won, he had to take me to dinner at the most expensive restaurant in Melbourne. If he won, I had to go to bed with him. I was so sure he could not win I had wagered my body. He never did collect, not because I welched but because he and my flight instructor died that weekend. They had gone to a flyaway and had done a torque turn, which is similar to a steep turn and the aircraft was a Bell 47—the same type they used in the TV show called MASH. It had already done a few of these turns but this time they went too far, pushed the envelope as we say, and it literally fell out of the sky and crashed and burnt. Both were killed instantly. You do lose a lot of friends when you are coming up the ranks. I have always accepted their deaths by, rather than talking about the individuals, but by passing a comment about the aircraft. Otherwise it is too personal, too close for comfort. These two men who were being a little reckless in a helicopter that I had many hours on (a Bell 47), beautiful aircraft that had the old wooden propellers covered, of course, with aluminium, but there was an inertia in the feel of the aircraft. So my lament was for the aircraft. It is only much later on that I discussed the individuals as people. We all find ways to accept death and rationalise it.

Chapter 17
Darwin and UK Application

My first foray from Australian shores was a job in the UK. I had been sacked by my boss in Darwin and decided to stay sacked. Everyone else turned up the next day ignoring their dismissal, but not me. I decided I did not want to work with the junior instructor. I must admit it had been a great job. While the boss was a legend in the Territory, flying was great. I was servicing the communities of Maningrida, Milingimbi and Lake Evella, which all added to my experience as a bush pilot. My aircraft broke down at Maningrida and I was billeted to stay with the school's librarian who loved living in the community. Having a strange female in town for a day was a good excuse for a barbeque. I had rung in and said I was safe and would expect the engineer on the Regular Public Transport (RPT) flight in the morning. I was told to be careful as you were not safe in the communities at night. I related this to my host and she laughed hilariously.

"Never had a problem," she said. I can still visualise her short fair hair, her fun personality and even remember her name—Beryl V. After denying any problems, she told of her first arrival in the community. She had arrived almost at the same time that the supply barge came in with its alcohol on board. Back then Maningrida was not a dry community, and it seems many decided it was a good time to celebrate not only her arrival but also the arrival of new supplies. She awoke the next morning and as she walked to her library/classroom she noticed that all the perimeter wire of the community had paper lining the fence. On closer inspection the paper lining the fence consisted of pictures from pornographic magazines. Adorning all the flat surfaces and walls of the buildings, were red-paint illustrations of male and female genitalia. Every night for the first six months she lived in the community, she had some local man come and masturbate outside her bedroom window and he also broke in one evening! But no, she had never had a problem. We laughed and joked about people's view of what makes a problem.

On a trip to Lake Evella, I had a flat battery. Here, I did something I got into huge trouble for with my boss. I solved the battery problems and jump-started the aircraft. In order to do this and access the battery, the same as jump-starting a car, I had to remove the cowls, attach the leads to a local gentleman's truck and then start the aircraft with the power transferred from the truck's battery. I must admit it was very scary re-cowling an aircraft that has a rotating propeller. He justifiably kicked my arse. I have, on more than one occasion, hand swung a propeller and thought nothing of it but you have to trust the person in the cockpit and you have to be quick. However, some years later I was in Vanuatu when I could not start the left engine on the Britten Norman Islander I was flying. I had landed, offloaded passengers, unloaded cargo and was all set to go for my last leg of the day when my left engine wouldn't start. I contacted the company on HF only to have them suggest I try hand starting. I just laughed, I said there is no way I could hand swing a motor of that size. So it was decided to send the last Santo flight slightly off track to bring an engineer and drop him off. By the time he had arrived I had already taken the relevant cowls off the engine and a quick check showed that there was no way I could have started it by hand swinging. He had a replacement starter motor and made the repair. By now, we were battling last light. As he was putting the cowls back on, I was readying for an immediate take off. While the communities are reasonable and we would have been made comfortable you could just about put a saddle on the mosquitoes and fly them home, so neither the engineer nor I wanted to spend the night away. We left right on last light as none of the villages have runway lighting, they are all grass strips.

***

Another friend was a Royal Flying Doctor Service (RFDS) nurse, a brilliant lady whom I know ended up as head of station in another state. She also spent time at NASA (yes, the space agency) where she was invited to study space medicine. Part of the RFDS job in these remote areas was to return a body for burial to the community it came from. All unexplained deaths in the Northern Territory are autopsied, so unless under the care of a doctor at time of death, the body is transported to Darwin where the procedure is carried out. Many of the undertakers in Darwin at this time were bigger rogues than in the cities. Especially, when dealing with the government who paid for the transportation and burial of the local indigenous people. So, as the pilot and my friend had to pick up someone from a nearby island, they informed another family that they would be transporting a body back to them for burial.

They duly arrived at the strip and landed. As the family formed a little honour guard to escort the coffin from the aircraft, the bottom fell out of the coffin and the deceased lay on the heavy cardboard that made up the bottom of the coffin. The family were so angry, they tried to kill the pilot and my friend. They ended up taking refuge in a tree, which the family then drove their truck into to try and shake them out. This went on for some time until finally, fuel low, they departed to refill the truck leaving the RFDS crew time to get out of the tree and take off. I never did find out what happened to the body.

***

So here I was in Darwin. Even out of work I had decided to stay in town as I had purchased a small unit right at Nightcliff beach. It was a little one-bedroom apartment. It had only cost 28,000 Australian dollars; I had a sea-view and the weather was warm. I was haunting the airport looking for a job, when I saw in *The Australian* newspaper (this newspaper in those days had an aviation page and all pilots looked there for possible employment) a job advertised for FOs in the UK on the Viscount VC8 series—a beautiful, beautiful aircraft. Not quite as large as a B737 but close to 30 tonne of weight. I applied and was accepted. I learnt later that they had over 200 applications and I was one of the ten selected. It helped that I had a father that had been born in the UK, and for me it was such a big step from a PA31 a Piper Navajo to a Viscount.

I had to pass the UK Commercial exams and the UK flight test. The test officers in the UK wear more gold braid that the captains of the largest aircraft or ship. They were so overdone and you could fail before you left the ground. The UK flight test was then impractical by anyone's standards. Beautiful sunny day and you had to declare that there was no ice or snow. You had to be seen putting your hand on the pitot tube and then state that it was heating. I know it is to satisfy them that you are aware of the conditions that can and do exist. I can understand if the weather is a bit iffy, then by all means a good check, but in bright sunny weather? A simple statement in relation to the checks lets them know that you know. Some checks are mandatory but to make you run a commentary simply because they are not paying attention to your actions is stupid. I was lucky, my test officer was a man who had worked in different countries and was a very experienced pilot. He had little gold braid, wore a flight jacket and put you at ease. As he explained to me, fly to the standard and you have no problems, don't, and you fail. I passed the first time around and was a very pleased female. One of the things that the British used to do (it has only changed in the last few years) is that, on short final you had to change the altimeter setting to QFE. During a go round one of the first things you had to do after flaps and wheels retracted, change back to QNH, QNE is only for flight levels. If you didn't do this, you failed. It is not so easy as this in a high workload situation. The Q codes were brought in I believe during the Second World War. The US still uses inches of mercury rather than Millibars or Hectopascals. As I said, they are not ICAO compliant.

***

One of our guys was ex-Royal Australian Air Force and an excellent pilot. I flew with him as my captain on more than one occasion and he was good, really good. However, on his test he failed as he got a lady test officer who wore so much gold—had it been the actual metal she would have needed more guards than Fort Knox! No, that would have been too heavy, but she was out to give everyone a hard time. This woman with a chip on her shoulder larger than Galloway Forest, failed our ex-air force guy, complained because he said, "affirm," instead of "affirmative." The correct word is actually 'affirm' but she was just a malicious bitch who wanted to fail this man or any man, because a) he was a man and b) he was an Australian. I ran into this same woman 18 years later and she still had the chip firmly in place, still working for the authority as a test officer and her reputation still precedes her. Just the other day, a friend who also worked in an organisation that used her, said to me she was called quite a rude name very similar to her actual name as she still instils fear in young pilots. I can only assume she had, at some time, failed herself and instead of taking responsibility for herself she put it on everyone else. There is a saying that those that can, do, and those that can't, test.

This is what I mean about having a regulator that follows the rules as set down by the regulatory authority and not people who have an axe to grind, whether it is of a professional or personal nature. I had such fun flying in the UK and much to my shame at this time, I had not been away from Australia often enough and I was an 'Ugly Australian'. These days the UK is one of my favourite countries. Being single, I was based at Aberdeen and the captains were lovely. When we were empty, we would fly slightly off course and I was shown the other islands that are close to the route to Sumburgh in the Shetland Islands. I was shown Scapa Flow and the German fleet that was scuttled there. When conditions are right, you can just make out some of the outlines of the ships. Scapa Flow is in the Orkney Islands. It was here I was taught to do a DME Arc long before they were in use in Australia. I returned to Australia to see family and renewed my ratings while I was there. My test officer said as he tested me "I am going to explain a new procedure we are introducing but you don't have to fly it." When he said it was called a DME Arc, I said, "Oh, I have been flying them in the UK, we use it to get into Sumburgh sometimes."

He immediately sat down and said, "Well then you explain it to me." And I did. He was most impressed. I must admit I think aviation is something the English do best. They have the best controllers in the world. Brilliant! We used to do a flight that went out of Luton. The aircraft was parked over the day and as we took off at Luton early evening, they were vectoring us on the track for final at Heathrow where we would land, to pick up cargo and depart again. It was usually around 12 minutes from taxi at Luton to engines off at Heathrow. Most departures seemed to be to the west and there was an NDB at or near Windsor castle. They always asked you to turn early so you wouldn't wake the Queen Mum. With that early turn, they would just destroy the SID (standard instrument departure) you were on, and your reaction would be to ask for a track. In all the time we made that manoeuvre, I have never known them to be more than one degree out, which was always quickly corrected. They are truly the best.

Another flight I did in July of 1989 before the wall came down, was in behind the iron curtain to Belgrade. The crew, apart from the cargo handler who came with us, were Australian. The cargo handler, I believe, was an Irishman. There was an air corridor that was a mile wide that gave access to these countries. We did a flight for the Red Cross taking much needed supplies to the city.

We landed and as the cargo handler opened the doors, he hung from the cargo doors a big sheet that had a large red cross on it. There was gunfire on the other side of the perimeter fence. It was a warm day and as we unloaded, I suggested we give the men working to get the goods off the aircraft as quickly as possible, some non-alcoholic drinks from the passenger bar, which they gratefully accepted. As we opened the drinks, they tried to stop us. When we handed down the coca cola, they were only the mixer cans. They wanted these unopened; they were going to sell them on the black market. We needed to use the facilities at the terminal and I must admit it was the strangest terminal I had been in. It looked antiquated, like some of the old-fashioned shops that populated Melbourne's arcades in my early youth, it looked much larger from the air to what we saw on the ground. The Viscount did have its own toilets but they needed to be emptied in a similar fashion to the mobile homes that seem to be everywhere in Europe during the summer.

Chapter 18
After Being Cleared to Line

My first flight after being cleared to line, was with a captain who immediately after lift-off, would go to sleep. As we approached 500 feet he would say "Your aircraft" and immediately fall asleep. It was so well known in the industry that one night as I was flying with him approaching a reporting point, when the controller who answered my call (yes, I was doing the radio as well, pretty quiet at night) said, "Evening Skippy" (my Australian accent earned me this name).

He used the captain's name who was asleep again and said, "You are doing both jobs of the pilot, flying and radio."

"Yes," I replied rather timidly, at least for me. But, in all my time flying with this captain, never once did I get to the top of descent and reduce the power setting, without him immediately coming fully awake, saying, "On our way down are we? What is the clearance?" And he was fully in charge once again. His behaviour gave confidence; you felt you were doing it all, but having that backstop if the shit hit the fan. He was my very first captain after being cleared to line and he really was asleep; you could hear him gently snoring. This man was a short man, so to be included in my list of favourite captains is unusual as many short people seem to want to make up for lack of stature by being bombastic.

Another captain whom I was flying with, was again a short captain. The English are not a large race. You only have to look at the armour in the Tower of London, and in some old pubs where you actually have to bend down as the ceilings are so low. Well, this captain was one of those full of bluster, "I am in command." CRM or 'Crew Resource Management' was a new concept.

Some still live in the days of 'I AM IN CHARGE', as one said to me, "I understand CRM; it means WE are crew, you are the resource and I am management." That would not go down well today. Anyway, we were doing Birmingham–Dublin, starting at 0200 hours for departure around 0300 hours. I was doing the checks and sitting in cockpit, checking that the correct track had been put on the flight director, having read the departure plate and had started to complete the checklist. The walk round had been done as the engineers are responsible for the pre-flight inspections and the general airworthiness of the aircraft. However, no captain worth his salt would operate an aircraft without having a walk around that aircraft before departure. I was once called in to work for an emergency. I was in Angola and as I liaised with the captain who was handing over, he explained his family had been in an accident. As I arrived to take over his flight in a Twin Otter, he said, "I have done the walk around, you are right to go."

I said, "No worries, but don't be insulted if I do it again as there is a part on the Twin Otter that if it is not secure, can and will kill you." So here we were at Birmingham and the engineer was standing out in the snow and dreadful cold weather giving the sign to start engine number four. For the Viscount (VC8), you started number four engine first as it had the shortest lead to the battery. Being up to the starting point on the checklist, I looked out the window and said, "My engines are clear."

This pipsqueak in the left seat, said, "They are my engines."

I must be slow as I didn't realise his rather mammoth hint and I said again, "My engines are clear."

To this he replied, "I say again, they are my engines. I am captain of this aircraft and they are my engines."

I don't suffer fools or egomaniacs and said with great distain, "Well, your fucking engines on my side of your fucking aircraft are clear. Do you want to fucking start or not? That poor bastard out front is freezing his balls off."

Dead silence and all of a sudden, a very quiet start four, I gave the signal to the engineer and we were underway. What a dick. I happen to know he flew with another female FO and had her in tears. She questioned his handling and she was right. He closed the power levers on engines two and three on descent, which was a no-no, as they gave airflow over the elevator.

She quite correctly questioned this, and again, "I am captain," while he continued to insult and berate her. That was one advantage of being a stroppy Australian. He never gave me another problem in any aircraft.

***

Because I was single and could live away from home, I was quite often based at other airports and spent many months flying out of Aberdeen to Sumburgh in the Shetland Islands; this was great flying. On a Saturday, they had one flight, which left early and came back in the afternoon. We were given accommodation at the local hotel and while we would have lunch there, we usually managed to get around and see the sights. We walked to Sumburgh Head and saw the puffins and there were some old ruins that had been unearthed and we investigated these. We went into Lerwick town and the most notable feature, or lack thereof, was that there are no trees on these islands due to the strong winds. I believe these days; this has been corrected with the building of shelters and that many gardens now have a selection of trees and shrubs that are quite lovely and hardy. This is where you see the Shetland Simmer Dim or endless daylight.

This was one advantage of my job—I got to see some of the most interesting places and events, such as the visit to the medieval weekend in Visby.

I did enjoy flying the Viscount, but again my big mouth got me into strife. I was flying with the chief pilot and he didn't like my attitude out of the aircraft and I didn't like his superior attitude. Ex-air force, he always put on leather gloves as he felt it gave him a better feel for the aircraft. There are still people who believe this. I find gloves, even the finest leather, take away my feel. On arrival at our destination, he made a remark to which I gave a short, curt reply. He challenged me and said, "You are being rude to me."

I agreed as I said, "Yes, but we don't like one another so why pretend? Do I do my job as FO correctly and have you any complaints about my performance?"

"No," he replied.

I said, "Good, that's what I am paid to do, it doesn't mean I have to butter you up once on the ground and off duty."

As I walked away, I said, "I shall see you at report time later this day." I have since learnt that such thoughts are best kept to oneself.

On this particular night we were doing Birmingham–Dublin, it was the first rotation of a four-leg rotation. First night, you would do Birmingham–Dublin arriving around 0500 hours, then after a day's rest you would do Dublin Birmingham–Brussels and back to Birmingham, where depending whether you had another roster of this, you either went back to your hotel or a driver arrived to transport you back to base. It was on one such night, when I was with a very experienced captain who had flown the B52 bomber. He used to be an FO on this aircraft for an American pilot who had married an English lady during the war. They were quite often asked to fly at air shows. When the American pilot died, the lady who had been married to him, asked Bill to fulfil the air show obligations for the rest of that year. Brilliant pilot, brilliant man, these men taught me so much. This night having almost completed our three legs, as we approached Birmingham it was obvious that fog had formed and the Runway Visual Range (RVR) had deteriorated below our landing minima. We had been informed that Manchester was clear, so we diverted to Manchester—to us a minor irritation as we were a cargo flight and had no passengers to consider. I love cargo for that reason—it didn't talk back, fight, argue or give the cabin crew a hard time. Just another diversion. No doubt our traffic guys were flat out getting accommodation sorted.

Airport Authorities have to arrange parking, stairs and transport from aircraft to terminal, while we pilots just land and put the aircraft to bed, everyone else is working flat out. Quite often, out of Brussels we had an extra man on board. This night we had also had this man. He was there to oversee the containers of nuclear waste we often carried. The UK was the nuclear dumping ground for Europe and to this day you could not get me to swim in the Irish Sea if you paid me because this was where much of this nuclear waste was disposed of. His job was, if we had an accident and crashed, to manage what happened to these containers. Yes, they all had the yellow sign with black skull and crossbones. I often laughed and commented, "My lovers would always find me, as I glowed in the dark." My casual attitude was brought home to me on arriving back at the aircraft once the fog had cleared. We needed to fly the aircraft back to Birmingham, where they had the facilities to deal with the waste. We were cleared through the airport terminal. It was obvious just how far from the terminal we were parked, as a car was needed to transport us airside to the aircraft. We approached the aircraft only to find the area had been made a no-go area, with danger signs and nuclear hazard signs everywhere. We took off and some minutes later we were back in Birmingham where they had the facilities to deal with this hazard.

***

Another of the captains couldn't do a crosswind landing to save his life and I was often given the aircraft even on his legs if there was excessive crosswind. As I had flown in cyclonic conditions and was famous in that particular country (Vanuatu) for landing on one wheel, then dropping the nose a fraction after first wheel made contact, then dropping the last one. So I got the crosswinds. This night at Wick the conditions were extreme—ice, snow and limited braking on the runway. I had done all my FO duties and been outside refuelling, when on entering the cockpit I was told to go and do his walk round as he sat and had another cup of coffee. I, who was freezing, said, "No, that is the captain's responsibility which is why they pay you 10,000 pounds more than me. Do it yourself, it is your responsibility." He reported me for not following orders. I had refuelled and filed flight plans for other captains, done their walk arounds, no problem; I was known for being reliable. Yes, I, like anyone else, make mistakes but tried hard and always discussed anything I wasn't sure of, with them. But to be told you are less than nothing, 'I am warm and staying warm, you go and do my job', that, I said no to and to this day would again say no. However, now that we have cockpit resource management, I doubt that would occur.

***

Chapter 19
Renewal and Orgasms

While in Aberdeen one of the company test officers came up to do my renewal. As we were flying the approach, the tower suddenly said, "We have an air ambulance on approach, go around and track to the north." I went around and made all the correct calls as per flight procedure, changed back to QNH (atmospheric pressure adjusted to mean sea level), gear up, flaps and set track. As the air ambulance was cleared to land, we were directed to come back inbound. I made the turn onto the new track and I turned the long way around which is the correct thing to do. There is a mnemonic for that very situation and when you are learning 'instrument flying' this is taught to you. It is O.I.L and means when tracking **Outbound** and need to turn **Inbound** you turn the **Long** way round on the directional gyro, and so I did. My test officer cheered and congratulated me and said I know captains that would have turned the wrong way. It was this ability that kept me employed and the fact that I could make an aircraft do anything I wanted it to. I became known as an extremely proficient handler.

***

After being in Aberdeen for some time, the company decided I should come home for a while and I was happy flying out of the different airports—one being Luton. I remember as I crossed the tarmac with a captain one night and it was so cold, I huddled deeper into my coat, pulled my scarf up and gloves on, the captain remarked to me that, "it was a lazy wind."

"Lazy wind?" I queried.

"Yes, it goes through you rather than around you." I even now have a giggle about that. At this time, there were scares with hijacks and bomb threats and it wasn't that long since Lockerbie. So as we entered the airports, we the crew, were often put through a far more extensive search than the passengers.

I saw captains empty out their flight bags and then say, "You wanted to see!" I decided to deal with this intrusion into our personal security with body searches by faking an orgasm, most took this in good fun because I always used to warn them, "Do that and I could get excited." Most just laughed, some cheered and even passengers cheered, all smiles.

However, this was to be my undoing and I got into very big trouble after doing this at Aberdeen. I had been at home, on time off, when the phone rang, it was crewing, they had problems in Aberdeen and I was needed to fly that afternoon. As I ran through Heathrow to catch my flight to Aberdeen, the security people had seen enough flight crew running for flights to wave me through, after a quick run through the machines I was on my way. On arrival in Aberdeen, I had ten minutes to make the flight I was to crew, when I ran into security for the flight to Sumburgh. All the passengers were moving through quickly when a very zealous female security guard decided to body search me. I have been body searched many times and I have never been searched as intimately as I was this time. Still clothed, but her hands and fingers entered my groin area with great determination. I questioned the thoroughness, hurried and all as I was, I thought that this was totally unnecessary and felt she was just coping a feel. It was explained that they had decided that pilots were a greater risks than passengers, as crew could have family that were being held hostage and therefore crew were to be treated as a threat. I said, "Hang on, I am an Australian so who has my family? My family don't know where the fuck I am. Do that to me again and I will fake an orgasm."

A couple of days later, she did it again and true to my word I faked an orgasm and she reported me big time. I was in serious trouble with management. This was used against me at a later date. Some years later, I was flying for another company and ended up in Aberdeen. A security woman—not the same one—came up and said, "Welcome back, we have missed your smiling face and the fact that your laughter used to ring through the terminal. Where have you been? You have been missed." I never said. But I hope that overzealous female got her comeuppance.

***

Chapter 20
Weekend Away with Cabin Crew

Another flight saw all the crew score a weekend away in Strasbourg, where we went to the local swimming pool. As we were topless, many young men surrounded our sun baking area and were lying there making tent poles in their shorts, much to our amusement. Having been told how the body, to Europeans, is just another body, we had asked if we were allowed to go topless. Doing so caused quite a lot of excitement. Cabin crew on these aircraft were excellent, fun and lots of laughs while maintaining a professional attitude with the most difficult of passengers. They were always cheerful, good for a laugh and I still have contact with some.

One of our stewards was as camp as a row of army tents. He was out of the closet far before it was popular to be. He was such a fun guy, always happy, nothing was ever too much trouble, a good man. I think it took more courage then, to be up front about sexual preference, than now.

He said the hardest thing he ever had to do was tell his mother he had AIDS. Yes, he was so far out of the closet, you almost wanted to push him back in, as he was so in your face. You had to respect him; he carried himself with such dignity and no apologies for being who he was. The saddest thing is that he did die from AIDS. The treatment available now was not available then. Everyone who could, attended his funeral. All the staff had such affection for him that they hired a bus so they could go to his wake, with the intention to send him off in style. The bus duly arrived to pick them all up for the funeral. The bus company had sent a bus not knowing it was a funeral or of his sexual persuasion. It was painted bright pink with fairies, elves and toys painted on the side. While initially horrified, they suddenly thought how he would have laughed and just gone along with it. So they all arrived at the funeral in this horrific pink fairy bus knowing he would have loved it.

***

I also met my first transsexual within days of arriving in the UK. I still smile with the memory of how I seem to attract a lot of people who have the most amazing stories. When I first witnessed this 'lady' walking past in the company offices I thought something looked strange but I couldn't work out why. She had very broad shoulders in comparison to mine, and I do a lot of swimming. Her hips were trim, her boobs large, and she had very large hands and feet. There were seven of us who had arrived together in the UK to work for this company, plus three pilots who had arrived a few days earlier. It was funny watching their heads swivel as they looked at this female vision teeter on the highest of high heels. I don't know if some of them already knew or if they were just impressed by the blonde hair and the small rear end.

Every year the company would run a duty-free flight for the employees as a Christmas present. I remember the day we arrived in Oostende, Belgium for our shopping spree and it was St Nicholas Day. We call St Nicholas 'Santa Claus'.

All the other people had teamed up for their duty-free shopping spree because they already knew one another. I was standing aside from the crowd when I heard a voice say, "Lesley."

I turned, and there was Priscilla in all her glory. At this stage, I was still not aware that this person was a transsexual.

"Yes?"

"Hi, I am Priscilla and like you I am on my own. Would you like to team up?"

"Sure."

So we started wandering around Oostende and one of the first shops we entered was a toyshop, and St Nicholas was there with all the little children lined up to see him.

Priscilla was looking at toys for girls. She finally purchased a rather beautiful doll and then some other toys for an older girl.

I said, "You have a daughter?"

"Yes, she lives with my wife."

"You mean husband?"

"No, I mean my wife."

Still the penny had not dropped. All of a sudden light dawned.

"Oh shit! Sorry."

"That's okay. That is understandable. I know you are from Australia and perhaps you are not up with the gossip."

"No, obviously not."

By this time I was transfixed.

"Well, I previously worked for ABC up in Luton and went on holidays as a male captain and came back from my holidays as a female a few years ago."

Speechless, I stared at this woman.

"Yes, that was a while ago and since then I have made the full transition."

"You mean, cut and tuck?"

It turned out she wasn't on her own really. She knew all of the other staff; it was just that she was not very well accepted in her guise and it was early days regarding this sort of operation. She had lived as a woman since first arriving back at work but the operation was still a way off because she had to go through day-to-day life as a woman for at least two years. That was the requirement back then. She had been a very good pilot, well considered by her colleagues, and yet when this happened, she was let go. She, apparently, was considered 'unstable'. She had been hired by my company as a captain, but it was then they demoted her to an FO as doubts were voiced about a person who would 'cut their dick off', as the other captains put it. You must remember that back then aviation was still a very conservative field to operate in. A very male orientated field and men could voice their opinions like that.

As we wandered around, Oostende we came across a photographic studio that was taking photos of people and then putting them through computer graphic to print the photo in black and white.

Unfortunately the colouring used in the photo seemed to enhance all the male attributes of her face and made her look very masculine. I remember she was very upset by this photo and she refused to pay for it. As we walked away it was obvious, she was visibly upset.

She said, "I didn't like those computer graphics. They did not give a true representation. I don't look like that, do I?"

Embarrassed, I mumbled, "No."

After that, we made our way back to the aircraft and a short time later we were back at Southend Airport in the UK.

That was the start of her adoption of me. I learnt more about her when she had to go up country to the flight simulator and wanted some moral support.

She complained about being discriminated against.

I commented, "I haven't been discriminated against."

"You're kidding."

"No."

In the end, she decided I must not be on planet Earth and that she had suffered major discrimination as a female. I never did tell her that I didn't think it was because she was now a female as much as it was for being different.

One day, she took off her wig and while she was on large doses of hormone replacement, such as oestrogen, they did not promote hair growth. I felt an empathy with her because she so much wanted to be a female. I didn't understand having always been happy as me. I know, I am not always accepted, but I simply don't care. I did understand the desire to be accepted, until I accepted me, I had tried so hard to fit in. Now, I don't bother.

At the time, I was sharing a house with five Australian males and she sort of adopted me because she thought it must be a smorgasbord come bedtime. She had made comment on what must have happened at bedtime. I just laughed and said, "We go to bed—our own beds, and we are too busy working on getting our UK licenses to be worried about extra-curricular activities."

One by one, we got our licenses and the house emptied, but not before we shared her company on many occasions. I learned all about gender realignment and I realise now I was not a very enlightened being.

The house we lived in had an upstairs and when we heard a car, one of the guys would surreptitiously look out of the top windows and before the bell rang and she teetered out of the car in her high heels, they had taken refuge in their rooms.

Someone would say, "Les, you get the door."

When she first started visiting, they did stay downstairs as there was lots of curiosity about her. They also knew she had a boyfriend, a young man who was in his early twenties. She was my age and I was in my mid-forties.

Conversations would mainly be about aviation but always it came round to, "Well, what do you guys do of a night-time, do you go to the aero club?"

The answers were always the same, "No, you already have the license, we are still studying for it."

She considered herself a femme fatale and she would banter and flirt, hence the posting of the lookout and the disappearing act on her subsequent visits.

I was directed to open the door and while being hospitable, I was issued instructions to get rid of her as soon as possible. This resulted in me gaining more knowledge on transgender operations than I needed.

One day, she actually offered to show me how neat the operation was. I declined. One conversation we had regarded her acceptance as a sexual being and the fact that in places like Saudi Arabia she would be highly prized. I have no idea why.

What she also shared, was her psychiatrist's opinion.

"My psychiatrist thinks that as I get older, I shall revert to my male tendencies."

"What does that mean?"

"Well, when I was male, I screwed anything that lay still long enough. I was a real stud and I loved women. My sexual appetite was rampant."

Stunned, I said, "But you wanted to be a female?"

"Yes."

"Are you nuts? How can you have it both ways?"

She confided that the shrink had told her she would probably revert and that she would like women again.

"Is the operation reversible?"

"No."

She giggled and said, "I guess I'll be a lesbian."

There were other conversations but that one was the most memorable between us.

Once, one of my housemates wasn't quick enough to make his escape.

He arranged the seating so that I was always between them. If I went to make coffee and sat elsewhere on return, he would find some reason to excuse himself and, on his return, once again, I would find myself in the middle. She was telling us about her aviation medical and about the doctor who had asked her if she was having trouble with her periods because she was on hormone replacement therapy. She nodded in the direction of her groin, "It just goes to show what a neat job they do down there."

My colleague, the eldest of the group, and by far the most mature, nodded and asked in a most serious manner, "What happens when you have an orgasm, do you have it as a male or as a female?"

She giggled, "I don't know. It just feels good." She batted her eyelashes and seemed to be coy.

While I have no real knowledge of this operation, she informed us (in layman's terms) that they basically fillet the penis and fold it back inside to fashion a vagina, and the penile skin is extremely sensitive, so the sensation is still there, only on the inside not the outside. The operation to remove her penis was irreversible and I wonder if this is the reason that the male to female transformation out-numbers the female to male transformation. The creation of a vagina is far easier than the creation of a penis. I also feel that physically and mentally they are still men. I believe it is a psychological problem.

She flashed a large smile and fluttered her eyelashes and said, "I really like men, I just can't get enough of them."

My colleague looked panic-stricken and thought she was going to jump his bones. He started making excuses about getting back to his study and how he had a girlfriend.

She asked, "Is your relationship serious?"

Clearly shaken, he mumbled something about that, "Yes, it is."

She went on to regale us that since the operation and the medication, her sexual appetite was insatiable.

I was really no help as I laughed uncontrollably at the obvious embarrassment of this poor male.

I really was waiting for a demonstration. But if that was the most serious comment the most senior representative of the household could make; I was pleased the others did hide away. Their comments constantly had me laughing so much, I ached.

***

The captains I worked with were no better and constantly asked me, "What should we talk to her about in the cockpit?"

My retort was that they should talk to her the same as they talked to me and treat her the same way they treated me.

They exclaimed, "Are you for real, she was a fellow six months ago!"

One morning, I was snoozing on the couch after a night flight when the doorbell rang. I opened the door and allowed her in but I was sitting there half asleep when she began questioning me.

"Why were the boys always out?"

"Was I jealous of her?"

"How did I feel that her figure was new and mine was surely starting to show the effects of gravity?"

Up she jumped, stuck her boobs out, and said, "Look at this."

I must admit they were bloody impressive. She continued putting me down until in the end I retaliated and said that she reminded me of that nasty Christmas present you buy for the relative you don't really like—you know the one—you wrap it with the prettiest paper and ribbons and bows—but when you get home you realise just how horrible the present is.

I said, "I believe that under her makeup, wigs and implants, she was still a fellow and still had a male brain."

Now I look back and know that it was not a nice remark. I should have been far kinder. In fact, I am far kinder these days and much less judgmental. In my defence, I had been flying nights and on arriving back home early in the morning due to a change of crew, all I wanted to do was sleep, I was tired. But for some reason or another I had dozed off on the couch and I did not respond with the kindness that these day I hope I would show her.

Over time, we had some serious talks. She was a father to a child and had been sexually rampant and was always on the make until around forty when the need for change occurred. Not all of us take change quite so literally. But transsexuals have to go through a thorough vetting process to make sure they are stable. They must dress as a female for a prescribed period of time and visit a psychiatrist for a considerable time to ensure that they really do feel like a woman trapped in a man's body, or vice versa.

This woman had been a captain and had gone on a break from work and come back to work as a female. That takes guts. When I first met her, she was complaining about sexual discrimination. She had written to a weekly publication, a flight magazine, and expressed her anger at being discriminated against. It must have been frustrating for her as she had been a captain on large aircraft and she was now having trouble getting any sort of position and when she did, her colleagues didn't want to be in a cockpit with her.

However, I couldn't let the discrimination accusation go and also wrote to the flight magazine saying that I had not been discriminated against, but then I had been a female all my life. To my shame I used a pen name because I thought she could end up being one of my captains, if she had the strength to prevail against the men at work. She approached me because she felt I must have experienced gender discrimination. At this time, I truly didn't feel I had been discriminated against. However, some of my friends commented sometime later that I wouldn't recognise discrimination if it got up and bit me on the bum. If it has happened and I don't get a particular job that I think I should have got, I just think they have missed out on a good pilot.

I returned to the UK nine years later and she was in the papers again for having taken another company to court for discrimination.

***

When the recession hit, the UK national pilots demanded that the non-UK pilots be dismissed and sent home to open up positions for more UK pilots. While most firms kept their experienced pilots, those that could be let go were, and this is where my big mouth played a part. Good pilot and all that I was, when push came to shove, I was let go to make room for those more compliant.

I was learning it was a shock to be out of work in a strange country and I buckled down to find employment. I applied for and got a job on a Brazilia which

I let go because I was also offered a position with a company in Wales on a B737. Unfortunately, the first gulf war started and the job fell over.

I returned to Australia and a couple of months later, secured a job in Fiji.

Chapter 21
Fiji, the Friendly Isles?

Arriving in Fiji, I was looking forward to working with a new set of regulations and flight conditions, along with meeting new people. Unfortunately, this was one of the worst experiences I have had in dealing with people even though I did get the occasional laugh. The whole experience was a fiasco from the start. The company did not get the correct visa and when I actually left Fiji it was decided I had broken the immigration laws. I applied to the Fijian government to have this accusation removed from my record as I felt that it could affect subsequent employment, which they did after an investigation which proved I was in no way to blame.

I often see Fiji advertised as the land of smiles, with campaigns showing dark faces with lovely white teeth smiling at you. In reality, it is not like that. Maybe if you go and stay at a resort, but to live in the city of Suva is a completely different experience. I arrived not long after another political upheaval and during this time the training captain had been thrown in jail, had all his clothes removed from him and was left naked. No charges were ever laid; it was just because he was white. The Fijians hate the Indians and the Indians hate the Fijians, but when you introduce an expatriate into the mix, they join together to make that person's life as difficult as possible. I would go flying with an FO and out would come a pornographic magazine. Along with that would be remarks like, "How about I come around and do this to you, after all that is all you women are good for."

My stock answer was, "Don't bother, if you need a magazine to show you how to do it, you can't be very good." I had more than my fair share of offers from these 'men'.

I lasted eight months in Fiji. About two years later when I was operating in Vanuatu, an aircraft from Fiji landed and a voice came over the radio saying, "Is that you?"

"Yes," I said.

The voice said "I am ashamed of how we treated you, no hard feelings, it wasn't personal."

I simply said, "Well, I have hard feelings and it was personal and if you were on fire, I wouldn't piss on you to put you out. I don't wish to see you, meet with you or accept an apology off you."

I cannot think of another country where I could have said that on the radio. But there was not a lot of radio traffic in Vanuatu and while I know everyone heard it, no one asked what had happened as they knew me to be a helpful happy lady who enjoyed my job. I got along with people and, as always, I did my best to treat all with respect, so for me to bite, it was most unusual. I was known in Vanuatu as Captain Grandma.

***

But the Fijian/Indian crew, were an undisciplined group of pilots. You could be given a level to fly at and if there was cloud at that level, they happily broke the level. I would ask, "What level was our clearance?" They would state whatever level we had been cleared at.

"Well, what are we doing not on our level, do you want me to ask for higher?" In the UK if you were only one mile off track you would be asked to explain why, any further infringement would mean loss of license. Not flying at your assigned level would have the same consequences. So I spent my whole flight time reminding them of being on level, which they ignored. Between flights they used to drink kava. This didn't make for a happy flying experience. Kava has a similar effect to alcohol on the brain; it is supposed to make you calm, relaxed and happy. Also, it apparently raises the blood sugar levels and many kava drinkers end up with diabetes.

I met one of the worst transgressors in Papua New Guinea. He stuck out his hand saying, "Good to see you again." I gave him a load of verbal and walked away. Other captains started coming to me regarding this man's alcohol problems. I believe he didn't last long. He used to consume a slab of beer a night.

Fiji had its own challenges. I had a bunch of Caucasian pilots who had no balls, no ability to stand up for what was right.

***

This captain, who had no flight training experience (training being the operative word), had this completely mad idea about flying instruments primarily on the Vertical Speed Indicator (VSI). The VSI is the most imprecise instrument of all the instruments as it has lag. This means it actually shows what is happening after it has happened. Considering the number of instructors who I have met, taught or interacted with, I have never met another person who uses the VSI to fly on. One day, I had to be checked out to fly to a particular island and he was one of the training captains. He was supposed to give a report on my flying—detailing how I approached the island, landed and my general handling. GPS was only just becoming known at this time and so heading and height holding was also an important part of the assessment. This particular captain gave quite a glowing report then qualified it by saying 'on this flight'. He could not say how I would behave on another flight. All respect for this man went out the window. If you cannot stand by your assessment, then you shouldn't make it. I was being assessed by this gutless wonder. The island we were going to was almost exactly to the north. It was a lone island, so far from the Fiji mainland that you only had enough fuel for one way. If the weather was bad you were stuck, as there was not enough fuel to go anywhere else. You did have about an hour of holding fuel, so you could fly round in circles for an hour and hope a chance arose to land. Refuelling was done from drums. Getting drum fuel to islands is expensive, so you try to limit what you take on board after considering weather and traffic. The day we went there was a beautiful, tropical, blue-sky day. On arrival, we were greeted with iced coconuts and a straw (coconut juice straight from the coconut stains clothing). These so-called friendly people were in no way friendly at all. While I had problems as a female, one night, the Chief pilot came knocking on my door. "Can you help?" he said.

"Sure, what?"

"The Indian crew are trying to lynch me! I am going to Nadi tonight to catch a flight home to Australia as soon as possible."

While you might think the story is garbage, I seriously didn't know if it was true or not. Yes, I did help him. For the next little while, I collected any mail for him, sorted bank accounts and generally kept him up to date with the state of play. Then the man who interviewed me for the position in Vanuatu told me that this Chief pilot had badmouthed me to him. What an arse! As for the hanging bit: Who knows. However, hanging does seem to be a recurring theme when dealing with Indians (again no names). There was another CFI who was also Sydney-based, facing the threat of lynching. He was working for the regulator, running a school which almost exclusively catered to Indian students out of Bankstown. Rumour has it that some students came looking to lynch him as he took their money and gave little in return—couldn't run a piss up in a brewery.

***

However, Fiji did provide cause for amusement. I attended an Indian wedding where the beautiful bride was bedecked with lots of gold jewellery. This, of course, was the dowry; if poor dad had many daughters, he would be beggared by the time all of them had been married. That doesn't happen if all the children are male. In fact, some Indian families resort to raising and dressing the third son as a girl from birth. The reason being that the eldest son inherited the farm, the second son went into commerce and that really didn't leave much for son number three.

We quite often went out to dinner and would go down into central Suva to one of the many restaurants there. On the nights we walked, my colleagues took great pleasure in pointing out to me that many of the prostitutes were actually men. I was quite disbelieving, as they were really very beautiful with no sign of masculinity at all. However, as we walked, we would often see men on the prowl and the ones in the know seemed to deliberately avoid the most beautiful ones.

During rainy season, we would arrange a taxi and got to know the taxi drivers quite well. My friends teased me about these 'women' because I refused to believe they were men. That was, until one night when a taxi driver told me a story.

He had picked up a Japanese tourist one night, who said, "Get me a girl. Take me to where the girls are." So, he cruised the red-light area, his passenger turning his head like a clown at the funfair. All of a sudden, he saw this very beautiful girl.

"Stop. Stop," he cried.

"That one."

The driver said, "No boss, that's not a girl."

"Yes, yes, stop. I want that one."

The driver tried to reason, "That is not a girl, boss. That's a fellow, who looks like a girl." The tourist did not believe him and allowed the very willing 'female' into the taxi. They drove to his hotel where the driver was directed to wait until he was ready to depart. Less than five minutes later the tourist flew down the stairs straightening his clothes, screaming at him to get him away because "the girl was a man!"

Some of the FOs did try to be nice to me that was, until other colleagues decided to bring them into line and try to get rid of 'the woman'. It wasn't much fun being ignored all day without any one to talk to.

Clearly, Fiji was capable of surprising the less-than-savvy sex tourist, and it could also be a very dangerous place. I saved a tourist couple from being robbed by some local con men. I rarely interfered, but I spotted this man and a woman and I recognised the situation for what it was and walked over to the group. I told the man that he was being conned and to get out of there very quickly. One of the conmen held the wife and the other held the husband. My intervention made the two local men very angry, but I stood my ground. On reflection, it was a stupid thing to do. I should have run like a rabbit.

I am not always the brightest bulb in the pack and I quite often act spontaneously, which has led to some scary situations.

I have seen thirteen and fourteen-year-old girls being dragged hysterically to their new home having been given to an old man in the tribe. I feel for those girls, but for me to have interfered could have resulted in a spearing or, as a Caucasian, eviction from the village.

So, I have also learned to turn a blind eye.

In Burundi (the Republic of Burundi in southeast Africa) despite their poverty, the disabled who are legless or who have had polio, all seem to have bicycles that they power with their arms. In Fiji, anyone with that sort of affliction is likely to have a little cart, like the ones mechanics use to slide under cars.

When I first arrived there, I had to go to the local hospital as part of my aviation medical. My boss's wife accompanied me. However, amongst the blood-stained walls she started to feel faint. She said, "I shall just pop outside and wait for you."

"No worries."

After waiting my turn, I exited the hospital and could see no sign of her. I looked around and noticed a group of people standing around under a large tree. Further investigation revealed two white legs surrounded by black and brown legs—I realised the white legs were prone. I rushed over to find her with her head between her legs. I eventually helped her up and got her into the car and drove her home.

She revealed why she had fainted. The tree she had stood under for shade was opposite the morgue. Here she had witnessed the arrival of three dead bodies. While one had arrived in an ambulance, the other two had arrived on less conventional conveyances. One was on a milk van; the body was in with the milk. The other corpse arrived in the back of a pick-up on a wooden pallet, and as it was transferred, one leg dropped to the ground. This caused blood to drain from her head and she came to under the tree.

My time in Fiji was painful for me because I felt that I never really achieved anything there. However, I did make some friends, including a young man who I played squash with three times a week, and he gave me, along with the others, a traditional Fijian farewell. We enjoyed a hangi (New Zealand Māori method of cooking food) and sat together happily eating and singing.

Fijians say that if you can't sing then you can't be Fijian, and I can attest that they do have the loveliest voices. But even these friends could never make it appealing enough for me to want to return.

Before I left, I was asked my opinion about the pilots' abilities. I declared that one would kill himself and his passengers if made a captain. Despite this, they did upgrade him to captain on the Islander (a smaller aircraft). Again, my assessment was correct, he misjudged his approach into Suva Airport, leaving wheel marks on the roof of a taxi, and ploughing into the ground well short of the runway. I take no pleasure in my prophecy coming true: they all died in the crash. He was an idiot who thought he was better than he was.

Chapter 22
Aurukun

After Fiji, I returned to Australia and was contacted by someone who had heard I was back and looking for work. That's how I ended up in far North West Queensland at Aurukun, and its associated Aboriginal prison farm. It was here I made new friends, people with whom I am still friends today. This is also where the snake incident occurred. Aurukun was a dry community where alcohol is banned, a stupid prohibition in my opinion, which only serves to increase the price of alcohol—for example, 200 Australian dollars for a small bottle of Johnny Walker. The white man is often blamed for supplying 'grog' to the aborigines to make big bucks, but it is the Islanders and aborigines who do the grog runs. On one occasion, they hired a twin aircraft and loaded it with grog. Impatient to return to their community with their booty they did not secure the load properly, despite telling the pilot otherwise; while the net was indeed over the cargo it was not tied down. Predictably, at take-off, as the aircraft rotated, the load shifted and they all died, the pilot as well. I lived in the community and got on well with the locals. I received a letter from them when I left, saying if I ever wanted to return to live amongst them, I would be welcome.

I met some real gems here, fine examples of country Australians. A nurse arrived and came over to introduce herself. She had a wicked sense of humour and it was obvious to me that she was going to fit in. I invited her to a barbeque and beers night, where we sat around a fire and she told me the story of her arrival in Aurukun. Knowing that life here would be a lot slower than in Cairns, a relatively big and bustling city, Carole had made her last night a big one. Lots of booze, lots of food and a very late night. While she had fun throwing caution to the wind, it was when her plane touched down on the hot runway that things started to catch up with her. I laughed as she told me about her desperate need to visit the 'thunder box', and winced at the thought of her having to hold on until she could get to her unit and 'let all hell break loose'. Of course, it being a beautiful, brand new unit for the nursing staff, its toilet had yet to be anointed by the cheeks of another. It was also lacking toilet paper. Being the pragmatic type, she had no choice but to use her freshly signed nursing contract to finish the job. As, she so delicately expressed herself, "I used that since it's the only thing it has ever been good for, anyway. They are not worth the paper they are written on, at least this one isn't, so I wiped my arse with it. At least it served a useful purpose."

We cracked up.

The head nurse was a gentleman and his wife and children lived in the community as well. His wife was a fully qualified doctor, but as the Authority did not employ her, she could not help in any way. I am not sure if it is just a ruling by the community health organisation or if she was actually accredited medically in New Zealand, but even in a life or death decision he was not allowed to refer to her. What absolute stupidity. But that is the bureaucracy of government departments. People say that 'the rules are the rules', well, I will fucking break them if it saves a life. The frustration of this situation must have been soul destroying for her. But her husband was a down-to-earth, practical man who, even in the direst of situations, shone through. He too had his stories, as do most of us who have lived in these areas, but while many of them had a serious side, he still maintained a sense of humour.

Before I arrived at the community, there had been a fatal plane crash, so bad that no bodies were ever recovered. As any first responder to these types of tragedies can tell you, the human body is much less resilient than the human spirit.

The community operated a C206 aircraft, a real workhorse that carries six people, plus cargo. It's known for being reliable; they say if you can close the doors, you can go. This is not a principle I have ever adhered to, but because of their reputation they are like flies in the Australian outback, wave your hand and you will swat one. Some locals had wanted to fly to Weipa, a small town north of Aurukun. Now, the C206 cannot put its flap down if the back door is not fully secured, if you can't lower the flap you cannot slow down. You can close it on take-off, but coming into land with the flap down you need the door locked. Well, not long after take-off the pilot had an engine failure, and while loading he had properly secured the door. He had no chance of making a low speed crash landing or of putting the aircraft into the smallest of spaces, as the panicked back seat passenger had unlocked the rear door thus stopping the application of flap. With no way of slowing down, they hit dense bush at speed and the bodies, of course, were obliterated, the only remnants, a finger bone.

When I first went to this community, the new Chief pilot had zilch in flying hours, he needed a special dispensation and was clearly threatened by my hours. He used to give me homework, things like beginning and end of daylight, which would take him forever to work out, so he could check my answers; now you can ask a computer but then you had to know how. I know that the earth revolves one degree every four minutes, so it was quite easy and I would give him the answers before he had finished working it out. Clown that he was, he decided to test me and check out my handling with a short field landing on the short runway at Aurukun.

He wanted me to land before the cross runway. The first time I landed I was nearer the landing end of runway than the cross of runway. He sat there and said, "Not possible, do it again."

So, I did. Six months later, he walked into the office and boasted that he had just done a short field landing, "pretty close to what you can do." I just laughed, I had no respect for this man and was frantically looking for other work, which, I shortly found in the Pacific island country of Vanuatu. Before I left Aurukun, I spent Christmas there and it was great fun. There was a black Santa Claus for the local children. The community dressed one of the local men up as Santa who raised lots of laughs as he just about melted, with the wet season making outdoors extremely uncomfortable. You do get used to it and after the community left the festive events, we went back to our own homes to continue with celebrations. I remember a group of us got together for the proverbial barbeque and drinks, I played some 'Kevin Bloody Wilson' discs; the famous Australian entertainer's Santa song is extremely crude and disgusting, but very funny. I believe one of our group was an ex-priest, but he sat there laughing along with us, tears coursing down his face. Come New Year, another day off saw us do some fishing. The barramundi is huge and a fish dinner sounded good. So, off we went, Pam, Martin, Phil and a couple of others, plus myself, only for our truck to break down. We had two community engineers on board, but even with all their knowledge we were stuck in crocodile country. The reason that communities have aircraft to service them, is because wet season makes roads impassable, and we were left sitting like sardines in a tin waiting to become crocodile food. Our excuse was, we were all new to the community and had arrived at about the same time. Once rescued we returned to the community with very red faces. I don't know why I was there, I prefer the salmon and mangrove jack to barramundi anyway, as it seems to take on the flavour of whatever else is on your plate.

***

Chapter 23
Vanuatu

Vanuatu has to be my favourite place in the world. Yes, I love where I live now, but I don't fly, you see, there are no real challenges. There, I could fly. I could scuba dive on days off and swim everyday if I wanted. Nothing like Fiji, where your house had burglar bars. In all the time I was in Vanuatu, not once did I lock my car or my house. There was no reason to, they only steal what they need and the only thing that had been stolen from me in all that time was my fishing rod. I am quite sure the Ni Vanuatus were curious as to how I lived and if someone wants to get in they will, so I never locked my door unless I was going on holiday. Vanuatu is cyclonic, but so were Fiji, Darwin and Port Hedland. I spent the happiest three years of my life there, and I only left because I was getting bored; if the visibility wasn't down to zero or the cloud was not low enough, I had no challenge. Here I had been taught techniques to get the Twin Otter off the ground in eight seconds. But I am smart enough to realise when you are looking for bad weather for excitement, it is time to move on. I needed a challenge. I had one man in my life at that stage and he thought he was Don Juan, trying to chat up my girlfriends. He got nasty when I dumped him. He asked me for a lift to the garage one night, and as we drove, he gave me reasons as to why I was being stupid for dumping him. After all, he had not succeeded in seducing my friends so what was I complaining about! On arrival, at the garage as I exited my car to see if his car was ready he grabbed me by the arm, prompting one of the local men to step in, a big man, tall and muscular, and probably of Polynesian descent (most Vanuatus are Melanesians and are smaller in stature, more like Papua New Guineans). That finished that. Lothario turned up in PNG and looked me up, but by then he was much chastened.

When I was in Vanuatu I was constantly at the maximum allowable flying hours for the week, month, and year. So, my boss told me I had to take holidays. I begged and pleaded, "No, I have already had holidays this year. Can't I be the standby pilot for a month?"

This should have all worked out, but as in many companies there are those who don't believe in doing their fair share, and two colleagues kept having sick days. My hours climbed even higher. In the end, I had no option but to take another holiday.

I decided to do it on the cheap and went touring Europe as a backpacker. I did seven countries in three weeks. I enjoyed Rome. I was in St Peter's Square and I could hear people making a lot of noise. I glanced around looking to see where the noise was coming from. I became aware of just where I was and noticed that there were lots of nuns and priests and people with their eyes steadfastly glued to a window. All of a sudden it dawned on me. The Pope was about to give a blessing. I laughed at how dense I can be. I really hadn't expected to see the Pope, even though I was right in the heart of Vatican City.

On my way, through the corridors that led to the Sistine Chapel, I was really surprised that there were so many works of art that were of a bloodthirsty nature. There were men depicted in battle holding the heads of the vanquished with bloody swords at their sides.

I joined a tour through the Basilica where there are pictures or carvings of all the Popes, and there are five blank spaces left. The guide said that legend is that when the remaining five are filled the earth shall end.

I found my way to a little church called John the Baptist in Chains and it was here that I saw the most beautiful sculpture that I have ever seen. When I feel I am standing in the presence of genius, I am moved to tears. In this marble statue, Michelangelo had depicted a nobleman and in the stone, you could see the hairs of the fur he had on the jacket trim. After seeing the sights of Europe, I headed back to Vanuatu.

It doesn't matter how much I travel, when I am returning home, I look at those making their way to the departure lounge and I think, lucky people, I wish I was them. I definitely have itchy feet.

Back in Vanuatu I resumed flying people to the different islands. One of the flights we used to make was to Lenakel on the island of Tanna where there was a live volcano that you could walk up to. There are eight volcanoes in Vanuatu that I know of, with some still forming underwater, the steam rising from the ocean to give away their secret. When I first started in Vanuatu, I was being checked to line, Peter, the chief pilot, took me down to Lenakel to check me out into strip, in those days the strip was shaped a bit like a basin landed downhill and then ran out of steam on the up side. There were many hotels and guesthouses, from there you climbed into a four-wheel-drive and went to the volcano. It was constantly active and it spat lava and grumbled ominously. Lois and Kelly were visiting me and I had arranged on my days off to take them down to see the volcano, Lois wandered around looking in, tentatively, while Bill sat on a rock wanting to smoke. When Bill asked the guide if he had a lighter, he took Bill over to one of the lumps of lava that had just landed near their feet and lit his cigarette with it. Bill yelled at Lois and showed her and they both took off down the hill as fast as they could. Usain Bolt would have had trouble catching them as panic or fright makes people do the impossible. I laughed; having been there before, I took it in my stride. But as Peter had told me, he was down there on the day of a big eruption which killed three tourists. He told me to never fly over the volcano, only around the crater and never below 3000 feet. He related how the day it really erupted he had been flying around the crater when suddenly a piece of molten rock the size of an aircraft flew past him. That requires some force. I think the natural wonders of the world, the power of Mother Nature, dwarfs anything made by humankind. In all the time I knew Peter, he was always completely honest with me and I trusted his advice.

One of the most exciting strips was Sara and it was at the thin end of Pentecost Island where the land narrows, but is quite high. Lonorore strip on Pentecost Island is where the bungee jump was invented, a rites of passage which involves young men jumping off towers with vines tied to their ankles. Should, on climbing the tower, they decide not to jump there is no stigma attached; they are still held by their loved ones and accepted. Only when they are ready will they make the jump. It is only in western society that we ostracise failure. I would rather follow their cultural acceptance instead of making someone feel bad about not performing. Such wonderfully accepting people. I had a neighbour who had come to these islands to teach these people about spirituality, I often laugh about that. Of course, others have tried to impose their religion on these wonderful people. The Mormons were there, 19-year-olds wearing Elder badges. They were kids, just kids. I have given the traffic guys at all the islands strict instructions that they were not to put God botherers next to me. We flew the Otter here, single pilot so the co-pilot seat was vacant, unless we allowed a passenger to sit up front. But they had to be briefed separately about not touching the controls. Also, with me, not to try to convert me to their religion. One particular late afternoon, I was taking off out of Santo when the young man next to me said "I am getting closer to God." I told him he was "about to get very close to God, as I am about to push you out that fucking door", (the cockpit had a door either side for the pilots to enter the cockpit if operating two crew). This young man gasped, "WHAT?" he said.

I repeated my threat, he asked me, "What's wrong?"

I said, "Nothing if you shut up," but explained that I will not be preached to in my cockpit.

Dumb bastard should have stopped there, but, no, he continued. "I have found something wonderful I just want to share," he said.

"How old are you?" I asked.

"Nineteen," was the defiant answer.

Having been taken to the cleaners by my family, emotionally and financially, I responded, "Christ! You haven't lived, probably haven't even been laid. Don't you dare sit there and pontificate, or I will throw you out." I meant it. He sat there in stunned silence for the rest of the flight.

I met his leader on another flight, and he invited me to dinner with his wife, I told him I had no wish to spend an evening with someone trying to convert me. He promised he wouldn't and I tentatively agreed to join them. I must admit they were very pleasant company, although he did give me the Book of Mormon as a parting gift. (The show of the book: rude, vulgar and well worth seeing). I also found that Mormons are just the same as everybody else as, when standing on the terrace of their unit in the Iririki Resort, the wife let go a silent but deadly fart. Gasping for fresh air I almost fell off the balcony laughing—good to know we all have gas, Mormons included.

The dinner was nice, but it seems that once your partner dies, the race is on to marry again as soon as possible, as if you die unmarried when you pass over, you are a servant, whereas if married you are a god. Both of these people had been married before, both have seven children from their previous marriages and I left thinking, *'Christ! Thank god I am an atheist.'*

***

Vanuatu has the best coconut crabs and they are considered a delicacy, once a week an aircraft used to go to the island in the far north—the reef islands. Here we would take on as many coconut crabs as our weight and balance would allow and every now and then a passenger would buy one for the family. Individual ones were always tied with string and I can't recall how many times one of these very large aggressive crabs would be loose in the cabin.

As they juggled the weight and balance so they could get as many crabs as possible they always made us late. On one occasion I had been asked to pick up an elderly man from the North of Espirito Santo as he was apparently dying. As I was approaching, I tried calling the traffic guy but they had already given up and gone home. All of a sudden, I was there and I had to be off before last light. One of the younger men ran up to the old man's home and piggy backed him down to me while the traffic guy installed the stretcher to its tie down point.

I gave the departure call and once airborne headed straight to home. A couple of nights later, I was talking to the Flight Service man at a social evening when he said, "You cut it close the other night." I was on the very north of the island with no high ground to the west and we still had light as I started the take-off run. What I didn't tell him was that I gave my departure call while taxiing for departure. I just laughed and agreed. I had circled over the sea to a safe altitude before I headed south for Vila and home.

***

One day when I was out flying, I heard on the radio a conversation between two of the company pilots. One of the senior pilots was saying he needed the afternoon off because he was seriously ill. The deputy chief pilot observed that he had appeared okay earlier that morning.

"What is wrong?"

"I am leaking brain fluid."

There was a stunned silence and after about 60 seconds, "Say again."

In a low but panicky voice came the reply, "I am leaking brain fluid."

"Symptoms?"

"There is fluid running from my ear down my neck and into my collar."

"Headache?"

"No."

"Vision?"

"Alright."

"Can you continue to Espirito Santo?"

"Yes, I will fly back to Vila."

I had finished my flight and I had the afternoon off.

Adam, the deputy chief pilot, said, "Can you hang around in case this is for real?"

"No worries."

On arrival back to Vila, a very embarrassed captain exited his aircraft, Adam walked out to meet him and he came back immediately, stifling laughter.

The headsets we wear sometimes for hours at a time, have gel pads that cushion the ear. It was this gel that had leaked and unfortunately the leak had been at the top of the pad and the gel had pooled in his outer ear, which had then overflowed and dribbled down his neck.

This was the first time any of us had experienced this and we did have empathy for the pilot. However, the story is good for a laugh and quite often gets told over a beer. This captain now flies for one of Australia's majors and so I will not identify him anymore than that.

***

It was also amongst these islands that I had the saddest flight. I had arrived at Santo and as I went to the crew room, I stopped off at the traffic counter to see what my load was like for the trip back. Sometimes we had to go into Norsup on the island of Malekula, it was a good strip and no problems were expected. However, the traffic guys were obviously upset, as I spoke to them, they said, "We may be late, Captain."

"Why on earth will we be late, I am on time, the aircraft is refuelled, no problems. So why?"

"The passengers are refusing to fly with the body."

"What body?"

So, they took me outside and here on one of the luggage trailers was this little body. I said, "Where is the coffin?"

"The parents can't afford a coffin, Captain, and he must go home to his island for burial."

Understanding their culture, I realised the need for him to be buried amongst his people. There are certain rites, which they believe the deceased must go through and so many days (sometimes weeks depending on the culture) after first being interred, the whole village gathers together to say their final goodbyes. This is when all the bunting is removed from the gravesite, but during this time there are ceremonies that span quite a period of time. Understanding the problem did not solve the problem. On talking to the guys, it seemed that they had decided to tie his little body to the bench seat that is quite often a feature of the Twin Otter. I had to explain I could not carry a body in the main cabin of the aircraft. Yes, we often carried coffins—a very different kettle of fish, as the coffin restrains the body's movement and muffles the noise.

"No, no, he cannot travel in the cabin unless he is in a coffin."

"Captain, his parents can't afford a coffin."

"Sorry guys, he will move, he could sit up, and he could fart!" Even their sad demeanour gave way to a stunned giggle, "No, Captain, he is dead."

"Sorry fellas, there is air trapped in our bodies when we die. So, we don't leak, all the orifices are plugged—and this trap the air in the body. As we climb, we go into less dense air—the air in the body expands and bodies have been known to sit up, burp, fart and have been thought to be alive."

"But he is dead, Captain."

Just then another Otter landed and I said, "I will stay here, I want you to go and ask the other captain about unrestrained dead bodies and climb to altitude."

He immediately said, "Captain Lesley is right, the body must go in the hold." Problem being, the Twin Otter had what is commonly called a hat shelf shaped hold. In other words, 'L' shaped but the shaft of the horizontal 'L' is weight limited. I suggested we use the passengers' luggage to build the bottom part of the hold level with the shelf. Put a protective cover over the luggage to protect it from possible leaks. We could then put the little body on top. But with rigor mortis having passed, the body was once more flexible. So, we got one of those grass mats that the women in the islands make and put his little shrouded body in the middle and folded it up around him, and tied it with shreds of pink nylon packing material. Having now sorted out the problem, the passenger boarded and we departed a little late, but with all satisfied, except his mother. I cried just about all the way down to Norsup to think of this poor little man in my cargo hold. On arrival at Norsup the mother attacked me as she felt I had dishonoured her son. The rest of the people pulled her off me and I continued on my way to Vila. However sorry about the lad I was, I felt I had done the right thing. Can you possibly imagine, had he done any of those things that I mentioned, she may have thought he was still alive and I would have had a riot on board.

Another day, I was asked to deliver an old lady who was going home to die. It was on a day when we had twenty take-offs and landings and so it was extremely busy. She was put on the aircraft at Vila and I flew the normal route, which meant that I went from Palma to Creg Cove on the Island of Ambrym. Her village was on the other side of the Ambrym Island.

The plan was that we would go to Creg Cove (Airport) and put off the other passengers and that they would then wait while we did a whole lot more airstrips and then two hours later, we would return to Creg Cove with a view to taking the passengers to Oolay.

As I approached Oolay, my heart sank, the strip had an elevation of 200 feet and there was a layer of cloud just above the strip.

On board was this very old lady who had waited so patiently at Creg Cove and I wasn't going to be able to get her home. So, after trying to approach from the sea and trying to get under the cloud and not being successful, I knew there was no hope of getting in from the base of the volcano. I had tried twice and it was not visible at all. After two attempts, we were supposed to leave but after Oolay there was only one other strip before heading back to Vila. I checked my fuel and spoke to the agent who said a slight breeze had sprung up and he felt that the cloud may disperse if I could just orbit a little longer. I couldn't see a problem apart from the fact that I had on board one passenger who was being transported to a medical facility and was extremely violent and there were four guards to control him. I thought this was strange as the medic had given him an extremely strong tranquiliser and I was told he would be almost comatose for at least the next three hours. I knew my flight time was no more than an hour and time on ground 20 minutes, so I figured I had plenty of time for a little more holding. I came around once again and there was this wonderful hole in the cloud; it appeared to be large enough to manoeuvre the aircraft onto final and land. The hole was perfect and as I touched down the old lady smiled; she had been so patient waiting at Creg Cove for the aircraft to take her home to die. As we departed the hole closed over.

One of the passengers told me she didn't feel she would last much longer. As her family came to collect her, the relief on the faces of all concerned made me feel vindicated for the time spent. The old lady was taken away in the back of a ute (pickup truck); it was decorated in a similar way to how they decorate graves in the islands. She was happy and smiling and pleased to be home. The Agent at Oolay said to me, "Captain, it just cleared, the cloud has just cleared." I continued the flight and at about 10 minutes out of Port Vila the medical patient started to rouse. The medication, while it was supposed to be good for three hours, was wearing off after just 90 minutes. The guards were restraining him as I landed at Port Vila with some tension as it was obvious, they were losing the battle; another day's flying was complete.

***

Another day, I was sitting in the cockpit at Vila when a male nurse came to my entry door. "Captain, are you going to Ipota?"

"Yes, that is on my run today."

"Can I give you this to deliver? We have a patient down there (it was a syringe already filled with fluid)—who you will need to bring back but we would like to start treatment as soon as possible. He has to be given this."

"Sorry, not in my job description."

"No, not you—we have a nurse down there to administer the injection, and we will be here to pick the patient up."

So, I duly put the syringe in my door pocket and all went as planned.

Setting off early one Saturday on a flight where you headed south to Tanna then back to Vila where you did a run to Santo but covering the Eastern Islands then a small run to the Northern part of the Eastern Islands at around 1300 hours, it was off to the far north to get coconut crabs. If you were rostered for this run on a Saturday you would do 20 take offs and landings. After getting the first couple of legs done, I was having a cuppa in the pilot's room at Santo waiting to be told my aircraft was loaded and ready to go. All of a sudden, I was informed the flight to the Eastern Islands was cancelled. When I first arrived in Vanuatu, I was doing the Eastern Islands when the wind blew up and my skirt was blown over my head. It was the first time I had worn a skirt and it had been at the request of management. I had always worn trousers as getting into and out of cockpits can be revealing. This was also the first day I had worn a thong. There was great cheering and great embarrassment on my part—they all knew my hair colour was natural—and I never wore a skirt again. At 1600 hours I heard my name being called.

"You are going now, Captain."

"But it is two hours early, what is going on?"

"We have been to the hotels, collected passengers and put full fuel on for you and the cargo is loaded."

Stunned, I said, "Okay, I am going."

They claimed that Vila had a lightning strike and the lights in both town and airport were out. I was told it was straight to Vila as I flew over Norsup, I heard a colleague call inbound to Santo. So, I asked the pilot to go to numbers. Most companies have a frequency where we can talk to one another.

To ask someone to go to numbers means go to company frequency, so once there, I said, "What's going on? I was told the lights have been knocked out by a lightning strike."

"No," he said, "the weather is not good. You will need to do an instrument approach." I turned inbound to Mele NDB; the ground speed was a bit erratic, I never got visual (which means I was still in cloud) as I went round.

I said to the tower, "Going round."

He immediately said, "There is a big hole, if you can find it you will be visual."

"Staying with the go around," I said, which is the correct procedure if you are in the clag. So, as I went around and came into wind, I have never ever seen ground speed drop so low. But I stayed on heading for the VOR again to do the approach again; if it didn't work, I would go back to Santo. There it was, the hole, it was huge and I was visual. Vila airport is in an amphitheatre so the weather can build where it hits the hills but here was this large hole—beautiful. I have never ever seen ground speed like I was experiencing in the aircraft. The Otter has a True Air Speed of 150 knots and on downwind with the wind behind me my GPS was showing 220 knots. As I turned base, I could see the very wet runway and realised there was a possibility of aquaplaning. I thought, *'I won't use brakes.'* I had also decided no flap, as the faster you are, the more control you have. As I turned final, the ground speed dropped right off, I had on a lot more power than one normally had on approach to land and just about 200 metres from the runway, the aircraft dropped a wing and momentarily, we were at right angles to the runway. I stamped on the rudder to get the wings level again and landed safely, though I was still concerned about aquaplaning.

"Careful now, no over controlling now, everything gentle," I told myself and as I went for reverse, I realised I was already almost stopped. I slowly taxied off the runway and parked aircraft. I heard my colleague call; he was cruising at altitude. I called him up and explained the technique I used. I have no idea if he heeded my information as he was extremely proficient himself. But you always try to pass on anything you think will help.

The passengers broke into clapping and cheering, while some ran for the terminal. Although our traffic men were standing out handing out umbrellas, a few passengers broke off and came to my door and shook my hand. The following day, it was declared a cyclone and my flight became known as the famous cyclone flight. I had passengers come up and say how rough it had been. My concentration was so intense, I had not noticed one bump.

***

I mentioned that the Otters sometimes have a bench seat at the rear of the aircraft; these benches are exactly fitted like a normal seat with armrests and seat belts. As no seat number are ever issued, only very tall or solidly built passengers head for these seats, as it gives good leg room. Far better seating for large people.

However, one day we were making an approach into Sola airport on the island of Vanua Lava and as we went for second stage of flap the aircraft showed signs of wanting to slide backwards. It literally felt like we were about to fall vertically on our tail. I reacted immediately by pushing thrust levers forward and called for flap 10 and the aircraft immediately corrected. This day I had an FO, as this particular aircraft was the only aircraft in the fleet without an autopilot. It was obvious we were tail heavy, not through cargo but through these three very large Polynesian gentlemen. I asked the FO to go back and get them to move one at a time further forward. A rear centre of gravity can have serious consequences for any aircraft but this was extreme. My FO Amy was a Ni Vanuatu and tiny in stature; she went down the back and ordered two of these men to move while I adjusted the trim of the aircraft. Trim is what keeps your aircraft level; by trimming up the aircraft, it climbs and by trimming down the aircraft, it descends. It takes all the load off the control column. As the aircraft regained level flight, we rejoined the circuit making a safe approach and landing.

***

I had been diving up at Santo and had dived on the President Coolidge wreck. We used to work six days on and three days off so I always used to dive my first two days off and then have 24 hours rest before flying again, as the difference in pressure can cause 'the bends' or decompression sickness. I had been in Santo just to dive the Coolidge and had my usual 24-hour break before returning to Vila where I was based. The aircraft arrived; I was travelling as a passenger to resume duties the following day. As the captain exited the aircraft, I saw him go straight to one of the propellers. He then came in with a worried expression on his face. He saw me and came straight over. "Come and have a look at this," he said. As we left the terminal to walk to the aircraft he continued, "I had a bird strike and it has put a very large dent in the propeller." He was right, I have never seen as much damage to anything as hard as a propeller. He decided he would not carry the passengers with such large damage to the propeller. He said, "Are you game to come with me? You could do the radio and help if I need to shut down the engine."

"Yes," I said, so it was decided we would take the aircraft back and he would come back in another aircraft to pick up the passengers. At that stage it was brought to our attention that there was a very sick little girl who needed to urgently get to Vila for transfer to a flight to Australia. On talking to the parents, it was decided that the little girl and her parents could also come with us to Vila so that she could be transferred to the jet going to Australia. The Boeing 737 was due to depart in approximately one hour and she had to be on it. We departed with just five of us on board, knowing that if it became necessary to shut down the damaged propeller, the aircraft would in no way be compromised regarding weight. In reality, these aircraft have such performance that they can continue to operate fully loaded on one engine. The passengers left at Santo were most grateful when they saw him return some two hours later to pick them up to continue their respective journeys safely.

***

There are many other stories regarding Vanuatu and the wonderful people there, flying and the friends I made. But the expat community was starting to get to me. Our pilots were wonderful people to work with except for one lazy bastard. While the rest of us were flying maximum hours each month, he was struggling to do 25. Thought the world owed him a living. I was bored unless facing really poor flying conditions, like the day the earth turned brown. A strong inversion layer was sitting at about 5000 feet and with the ash, smoke and fumes from the volcanos (there were seven or eight just in our area) all caught under the inversion layer. The engines were pressure washed every week, as we were flying in an atmosphere laden with salt and sulphur from the ocean and volcanoes. The traffic men would lie to us saying, "Rainy go down small," when it was still bucketing down, causing pools to form on dirt and coral runways. It made landings hazardous. I was bored and decided to look for a position elsewhere. I applied for, and got a position in the UK and so could use my UK license again.

Chapter 24
Back in the UK

I love the UK. The aircraft are well maintained, the weather is sometimes a challenge, and the radio always a challenge as it is so busy that you use the slightest gap of silence to give your call. Busy, busy, busy. The Civil Aviation Authority leaves you alone as long as you comply.

Ah, the magic of theatre! Oh, how I love English theatre, the best theatre in the world. With some quite big American stars traversing the pond to act on a London stage, I saw Patrick Swayze in 'Guys and Dolls', David Soul and many others. Another advantage of English theatre is that you also see some of the actors on stage that we usually watch these days on the silver screen. I can never think of Judy Dench without picturing how petite this lady is. I saw Edward Fox in 'A Letter of Resignation'. I was so in awe of his brilliance in his portrayal of McMillan, the Prime Minister, at the time of the Profundo Affair, that I was in tears as I felt that I was in the presence of genius.

***

So, having secured a new position in the UK, I stopped in Brisbane to visit my parents as they had retired to the Gold Coast. I said, "hello/goodbye," and was on my way. On arrival, I was greeted with the news that the company had lost three contracts and I was no longer needed. As I pondered my options, one of my colleagues suggested I return to Vanuatu as I had got on so well with everyone.

But one of my UK friends said "Stick around, there is so much work, I am sure you will get a job."

I got three on the same day. I picked the first one who rang, which even then felt like a mistake, as management was busy stripping assets. The finance manager had new cars for both his wife and his girlfriend and there wasn't a member of management that didn't have an ulterior motive. But it was a job on the Shorts 360 (SD3-60.) It had a variety of names—one was the 'flying shed' as it was like a box with wings. Others called it the 'Irish Concord'. What an insult to the concord! I always felt that the aircraft was one of the prettiest aircraft ever built, such lines! Whereas the SD3-60 was, definitely a box with wings. But every surface of it produced lift and it was a very versatile aircraft. Crosswind landings could be tricky as with the large fuselage it often 'weather cocked' on landing. The cockpit, however, was well set out, large and comfy. I must say the

English couldn't build an aircraft if their life depended on it. Oh yes, they have the boffins—the people with brains—but having the idea and executing it are two different things. The two examples that spring to mind are that in the old Viscount, instruments vital to the captain were on the co-pilot's side—the ignition/starter for one. One captain used to carry a large stick so if he needed something and you were tied up with radio, he would use this extension to move levers, press buttons and generally get the job done as much as possible without help. As one captain said to me, 'they built the aircraft and then realised someone had to fly it—where shall we squeeze the pilots?' The Harrier jump jet—another fantastic piece of machinery, but first production saw them forget to put in an instrument landing system and the joke was you could tell a Harrier pilot by the crick in his neck. There were red faces when someone asked where the glideslope was, too. It was subsequently added on to the instrument panel. So, to fly the glideslope the pilot had to crane his neck and constantly look down, hence the crick in the neck. Now the US, when they design an aircraft, they put two seats in first then design from there. However, it is British ingenuity that designs the best aircraft. So, while I have no idea who designed the SD3-60 it very definitely looked cumbersome, but was not only comfortable but a delight to fly.

I made contact with my former landlady to enquire about my old room. I asked if she still had the room available and yes, she did, however, she had changed jobs, she now worked in a brothel. I said "At your age?!" She assured me she was one of the most sought-after girls who worked there. I must admit she was an extremely pretty woman. One morning, I was downstairs making coffee (I lived upstairs in the attic). Scarlet came in with a huge grin on her face. Wednesday night was the night when she had her toy boy in. He was less than half her age, being in his late twenties, and she was sixty at the time. His father owned the luggage shop at the local markets and he had bought himself a cheap shirt there. It had cost one pound. It was royal blue in colour and very vibrant and looked quite smart. It had been a hot humid day in the UK, by English standards and he had been perspiring. Unfortunately, the dye in the shirt had run onto his lilywhite English skin and she said that as he walked around his side of her bed, he looked like one those South American toucans with a bright royal blue chest.

He hopped into bed and she remarked, "It was like having sex with a passionate parrot."

Scarlet often came home with fists full of pound notes. She tells me she was one of the higher priced girls. Not long ago, I was watching television and a show came on from the UK about granny call girls. There was an 83-year-old woman saying how much she just loved sex! Oh well at that age I guess you are as grateful as hell; you probably don't yell and for sure you don't swell.

She did have individual ones who came to the house. I didn't care, it was her business and I lived upstairs so I heard nothing. One night I was not quick enough to make my getaway and I met one of her younger clients. He had obviously asked about me because I had answered her phone to him. He knew I was a pilot and he worked in the aerospace industry at an extremely large company that customised large aircraft for private customers. He offered to show me around the factory. One evening, I met him for dinner and then we went to visit his workplace. He showed me through a B747 which had been stripped bare; the interior was being made into a flying home. Upstairs, above the rear toilets there were sleeping quarters for the cabin crew and the main area was to be bedrooms and lounge rooms and bathrooms. I was surprised when over the course of dinner, he cried his heart out to me about wanting to make Scarlet his one and only. He thought I might be able to talk to her. This was something I kept well out of.

She came home late one night and plopped on the lounge, "I am exhausted, I have done eighteen today."

I said, "Full sex?"

"Oh no, I had three spankings."

I laughed and laughed.

I also learnt that water sports were not necessarily about going to the beach and playing with a Frisbee. My knowledge was broadened and I stayed upstairs and out of the way when her private clients turned up.

***

The airline was the usual company with people playing political games and I quickly realised I had made a mistake in joining them. However, I had signed a contract promising to fulfil an 18-month stint. We sign contracts, some include bonds as they are going to the expense of type rating you, which means it costs them to give you an endorsement to type and for that they want blood. I have yet to read an aviation contract that is fair, as my nursing friend said all those years ago that they are only useful when short of toilet paper. They all favour the employer and it is just another way to screw the pilot. Why do we sign? Well, it is nice to get paid and you don't get the job if you don't sign the contract, stuck between a rock and a hard place. Only once has a contract worked in my favour. I was working for a Chinese flying school in Western Australia and they decided to withdraw a promised monetary advantage because of my age. At that particular stage I was studying law in my spare time and that semester we were studying contacts, and like most universities we had study groups. My group needed an actual contract to study so while we were perusing said contract, there on approximately the third clause was written 'during the course of employment these are benefits to be paid to'. The company had suddenly and without warning removed a financial benefit to me. This clause was brought to their attention by me and it was duly reinstated as I pointed out that if they could remove that benefit the contract was null and void and I could leave immediately.

I was working out of the north of England amongst the Geordies and we did a regular run in the SD3-60 to Belfast City. I really like the Geordies as they have a wry sense of humour and while I enjoyed the flying, I did make friends and the following is a story about my friend, with whom I was enjoying a coffee when she told me about a recent night out.

She was going out for the night with her husband and another couple to a gala and they were all dressed up in finery; ball gowns and dinner suits. Her friend's husband was a vet.

Just as they were about to leave, his phone rang.

He said, "We have to stop at Mrs Mac's house on the way—she is a dear old lady and she has called and told me her old cat Tiddles is very sick. I have been treating him for cancer and have told her I will probably have to put him to sleep."

They all agreed that they should make the house call.

When they arrived, all dressed in their finery, it was clear that poor Tiddles was too sick and would in fact need to be euthanised.

The vet told Mrs Mac, "I will have to take him with me, he cannot be helped now. I will take him with me and ensure he gets put down humanely."

He took Tiddles in a basket and Mrs Mac said farewell to her beloved cat.

The vet had come straight from home and not his clinic, and there was no time to return to the clinic before the Gala. He discovered that none of his small animal equipment was in the car and he only had a captive bolt pistol, the kind used to kill larger animals such as cattle.

There was a hedge in front of Mrs Mac's house so undercover of the hedge, they held Tiddles on the road and the vet fired the pistol.

"Oh my God, the bolt had gone right through! He is bolted to the fucking road!"

It was true, the cat's head was well and truly entrenched in the road and could not be moved, and they were right out the front of the house.

There was mad panic as they tried to pull the feline free. Some of the cat came away but the head remained firmly in the bitumen.

Linda raced to a neighbour's house where she managed to procure a shovel. They used this to leverage poor old Tiddles off the road. They were a little late, but the gala was a success.

While some of our flights were charter, the regular RPT was to Belfast City and I had to learn how to conduct a search for bombs. Belfast City Airport is a very secure airport but it was always better to be sure than sorry or dead. Anytime we had an overnight we stayed at the Stormont Hotel opposite the Parliament of Northern Ireland. We stayed here as it was one of the places that did not have a barricade between the hotel and the airport. So, we would have to inspect the aircraft for all the places that they could secret an improvised explosive device. The SD3-60 had a sort of mudguard over the wheel and this was a particular favourite amongst the IRA, or so I was informed.

One day I was talking to a colleague when he informed me, he had been the captain of an aircraft that had been hijacked. The gentleman was an Iranian and had been flying a Boeing when he was hijacked. As we talked, the whole story came tumbling out. As he finished, he said, "I have never told anyone else that," and I am sorry to say with his accent and his trauma, much was garbled. What I did understand was that he had spent hours with a gun pressed to the back of his head. In those days we use to squawk a particular code on the transponder that would tell when we were under duress. So, as they tried to get clearance to land at airports in countries the hijacker wanted, they were refused clearance. In the end he told the airport they were now planning to land as they were on vapours. Although there were trucks and barricades on the runway he was landing anyway as he had no further options. The runway was miraculously cleared and on landing, negotiations began. No doubt he did his best to keep everyone alive but in front of him one of these arseholes shot a passenger. I will always remember the anguish on his face as he related his story to me. You go off to work to a job to which you have full commitment, weather, aircraft acceptability, traffic, crew for whom you are responsible and someone decides they are going to kill people just because they can. I know two wrongs don't make a right but I believe we should just do to them what they were trying to do to us. No sympathy, no do-gooders, no one saying their belief system is different. You come to live in our country, you live by our rules. Not us by yours; when we go to your countries, we are expected to live by your rules so what is the difference? I will never forget how that man, who was just doing his job, was left in so much pain.

***

It was in the UK that I made the worst mistake in my aviation career. I was flying with a very nice man who was the captain on this flight. He had a great sense of humour, was honest and an all-round good guy. He left me to work out the fuel for the flight. The weather had been bad and I had arranged holding fuel reserves and 'some for mum' as the load was under what we could take. Just insurance, was my thinking. On arrival at destination we were asked if we needed to refuel, I said no, having made sure we had plenty when leaving from our departure airport. However, I had made an arithmetical error and we actually had less than the required amount. Once airborne, the captain checked my figures and he queried my math. I am usually so good at such calculations neither of us could believe what I had done. The gods must have shined on me that night as the weather cleared and we made the return flight landing with our reserves intact. I have never made that error again. He did growl at me as we departed that night at the end of my duty. It was not a passenger flight but freight, but it should never have happened and I was remiss. I do admit it was one of my last flights before leaving for Australia to see my father before he passed. But no excuses, it was a big, big mistake we were just lucky it turned out as it did.

***

The company decided to expand into jets and I immediately thought 'time to move on'. I had enjoyed the area, there is a wonderful little theatre in Newcastle upon Tyne. I had explored the area and visited Holy Island and the beauty spots of Scotland that were closest to the border. I always made time, every week, to ring family and was informed my father had cancer. I decided I would head home and put in my resignation. I gave the required three months, knowing that the company would be closing its doors within the next 12 months. As the jump from operating turbo props to going to jets, whether they be state-of-the art, new whiz bang all singing and dancing jets, or just some older type that larger companies were replacing with more up-to-date equipment, the learning curve is enormous. Management in airlines are usually not aviators, engineers or anyone who has any idea of how to plan, schedule or efficiently run an aviation organisation. You say a CEO can manage anything—a bean counter can count beans, doesn't matter if the beans are green blue or red. But in reality, it doesn't work.

I have heard that one Australian company was saying no to experienced pilots in order to hire people with less experience, as they wanted a blank sheet to work with. Crazy, I know so many Australian pilots at the moment flying for a particular company in the United States where they are valued members of staff. When I first went to the UK, I was at 47, considered too old in Australia. The English look at my total hours and see experience. So, management decided this company, which had been successful for many years, was going to diversify into jets, and they closed their doors around 18 months later, as so often happens.

While serving my notice, I received a phone call from my mother that I was to come home immediately as my father was not going to last the weekend. I remember being very surprised because I had always felt he would die in September, which was why I had resigned in June—it had been a feeling but a very strong feeling. So, I jumped a flight to Australia and while I could not get direct to Brisbane, I managed to get to Sydney and then jumped a domestic to Brisbane. I walked into the hospital and here was my father sitting up in bed saying, "What are you doing here?"

I returned to finish my resignation three weeks later with Dad still hanging on.

Once or twice, it was really brought home to me, how when he had a problem, he would ask me to sort it out. I was the logical, common-sense daughter, no frills, no dramatics. It was this he needed and both he and I understood the need for him to depart. He had been thrashing in pain one night and knocked over some water and the nurse chastised him like he was a naughty boy. He said, she spoke to him like he had a screw loose. He was looking to me to protect him.

I went to the nurses' station and explained, "Please don't talk to him like a child, he is fully aware—he hit the water jug as he was in pain and it was an accident."

The nurse apologised and said she would speak to him and to tell him when the pain got so bad, he should ask for help with it. She was lovely and she built such a rapport with him. On one occasion she told me to tell him how to exit his life. I did pass this on and had asked that he be marked as do not resuscitate. She had approached me as she felt she could talk to me where neither, my mother nor sister would accept the inevitable. In the end, I left and returned to the UK, he waited till my mother left with her promising to visit next day, but by the time she drove home, he had done what I and the nursing sister suggested.

Chapter 25
Fantastic Sweden

While I was away, I had applied for a position in Sweden and was successful. What a marvellous country and people. Interestingly, there is no Swedish massage in Sweden. The flying was wonderful and it was a whole different ball game.

In the UK and other countries, you do your approaches to the individual lights; in other words, if you are flying in low visibility, when you get visual you must be able to see individual lights. But in Sweden if you can only see a glow, you can continue. We did a lot of low visibility approaches with the FO flying the approach and the captain taking over at becoming visual. This method is for safety because the captain remains with his eyes out of the cockpit while the person flying the approach remains with his eyes locked onto the instruments. The theory is that the transition from instrument to visual flight, when you only have seconds to go, is too much for the brain and eye to react, therefore the handover from FO to captain is the normal procedure.

I had experience with flying in cyclones but the ice build-up demanded a whole new set of skills. When do you put on the de-icing equipment? These were all new and interesting skills to learn.

It was in Sweden that I tried tobogganing and some of my exploits became fairly wild. Once, on a run, I became airborne and landed in a tree but luckily was uninjured. Soon after that, I was out walking and fell. I sustained a compression fracture on my wrist. Go figure.

The medical care in Sweden is wonderful and the doctor had me sorted out in no time without surgery or wires, even though it was an extremely bad break. He did have to pull it into place twice to get it perfect but in doing so he told me it would be a complete fix. And it was.

One evening, I arrived back at Sundsvall and it was the coldest temperature that I have ever experienced. It was minus thirty and the FO and I were all rugged up as we tied the aircraft down for the weekend. Every exposed part of us hurt. We had to remove our gloves to put knots in the ropes to secure the craft because the aircraft was not put away at night-time. I had been told that where the tyres make contact with the tarmac, they freeze and so when you taxi that part of the tyre is flat and so the taxi is a bit clumpy as the flat part of the tyre comes around. This did not happen to me, but it does get very cold and further north than Sundsvall, they put the aircraft into hangars overnight. I had to decide when to have snow removed from the fuselage before a flight and one day met with some resistance from one of the men.

He said, "What makes you think you can handle these conditions?"

I responded, "Well, I have close to 10,000 hours and have flown all over the world, and I may not have flown with ice like this but if you had come to my country, I would not be so judgmental. I figured the company would make sure I was correctly schooled in icing procedure and landing on contaminated runways and I would give you the benefit of the doubt, at least until you stuffed up."

It wasn't hard to determine if an aircraft needed de-icing. Just blow on the snow, if it blows away, it is powder snow and dry so does not adhere. If it does not blow away then you have to have it removed with de-icing fluids that are not very environmentally friendly.

At Hudiksvall, we had a de-icing fluid that was not as efficient but was much safer for the environment. In Arlanda, they used what was called 'fluid type 4' and you had to taxi to a specific area of the airport to use it. With other types you had to be airborne within so many minutes of it being applied to be effective.

Landing on snow was not as scary as I first thought. Braking is limited depending on the conditions but I found the whole experience worthwhile. I ended up training an ex-Swedish Air Force captain (not used to the slower turbo prop) and as we were flying along and our airspeed was decreasing, he remarked,

"We have a strong headwind."

I said, "No, we have ice build-up."

He argued with me. He had been flying a SAAB fighter jet, the Gripen. These aircraft are so fast that ice doesn't have time to build up on them as they go through the icing layer, so no doubt he felt sure of his facts. I, on the other hand, reached over and switched on the ice light. This light shines right on to the surfaces that are impacted with ice and as we illuminated the leading edge and propeller, we could see that there was a large accumulation of ice.

Oscar could not understand how this was making a difference. I had been castigated by some members of the crew for not fully understanding Swedish flying conditions, according to them. Yet here was a man who had grown up in Sweden, flown in Sweden from the beginning, and didn't understand ice.

I had just reached over and put on the de-icing equipment when suddenly the airspeed started to increase. This was because we had just got rid of the excess weight of the ice and this increased the laminar airflow across the wing. You do not put on the de-icing equipment until you have a build-up of ice otherwise it can just deform its shape. There needs to be enough build up so that the de-icing causes the boots to expand and breaks off the ice. The boots are an inflatable rubber and they expand when activated which causes the ice to break free.

I never spoke of the matter again but I know Oscar learnt a valuable lesson that night.

***

I go back to Sweden nearly every year, and every year there is a group of people who want to see me. While I was in Sweden, I did a lot of travel, both within Sweden and to nearby countries. One of these countries was Russia and I found myself in Moscow. What a beautiful city. It is called the city of a thousand golden domes.

I had always wanted to go to the church in Red Square. I always called it the onion dome church, and it is really exquisite. Upon entering the church, I found the steps extremely high. I am a tall woman and I struggled to get up these very high steps. On reaching the top, a guide told us that the steps were high so that the parishioners would be in awe of the priests and God because they would assume that they walked up these stairs with no effort whereas a common man struggled mightily. The priests have a different entrance where they walk up normal hidden stairs.

Walking around Moscow on a Sunday, people were doing what we do on a Sunday; they were having picnics in the gardens surrounding parts of the Kremlin, eating ice-creams, laughing, and playing with their children. I thought, they like all the same things we do. For how many years were we fed propaganda about the Russians? We were told that they were something to be frightened of, and worse, communists. But the man in the street has the same loves, desires and worries that we have.

I was standing in Red Square when a young woman approached me and asked if I wanted to do a tour of the Kremlin? We bartered for a while before agreeing on a price and I stupidly asked her how she knew I was a tourist. I say stupidly because in retrospect I remember I had my 'Shaun the Sheep' backpack on, as if that wasn't a neon sign saying, 'tourist'.

The tour of the Kremlin was remarkable. As you enter, the home of the Bolshoi ballet is on your right. Within the walls of the Kremlin there are five cathedrals dating back to the tsars. One cathedral had a floor made entirely out of semi-precious stones; onyx and tiger-eye. How magnificent. There were icons on every wall of the cathedrals and I was told that the third icon from the main panel tells the name of the church; this was because most of the peasants were illiterate.

In one of the cathedrals, I noticed a piece of needlework that was very fine. A monk had made it and it was of a woman who was wearing a dress. The stitching showed shading, in the folds of the depicted dress, it was exquisite. I do not think that sort of needlework is made these days. It was really beautiful.

The tour by this young woman, who spoke very good English, started from the moment we agreed on the price.

She said, "Have you heard of Lubyanka Prison?"

"Yes, I read about it in a book once."

"It is down the end of that street," she gestured to the street alongside the Gumm store.

We purchased tickets to enter the Kremlin and the flag was flying, which meant that Putin was in residence.

We looked over the largest bell ever made, but it had never been rung because it had been badly cracked while being made.

Then I was shown the largest cannon and cannon ball ever made; again, they had never been used, as the cannonball was so large it could not be lifted into the canon for firing. It almost seemed that Russia applauds its failures more than its successes. Then we went to some of the cathedrals.

I was completely amazed by the pieces on display and the richness and opulence of the whole place. I found the people friendly and even though I couldn't speak the language someone would see me studying a map and come over to help. I would point to where I wanted to go and they would point to where I was on the map and so I could work out how to get there. One old gentleman actually took me by the hand and led me to where I wanted to be. I often think of this old Russian gentleman who was open and kind enough to take the hand of a foreigner who spoke no Russian, and guide her to where she wanted to go. I think how I had to overcome my own fear by having the trust to follow him. These people are not really so different from us. It is our fear of difference that causes problems.

Moscow was excellent. I stayed at a trendy tourist hotel which was only five stations from Red Square; I sat on the train and counted the stations. After a couple of trips, I got to recognise which station I was at because of the architecture. The station where I boarded the train was big and airy. There was another one that was all marble and the one at Red Square had huge statues of workers holding hammers and sickles. Russia is almost worth visiting just for the train stations, at least in Moscow.

Each floor of the hotel had its own concierge who noted your comings and goings. I am sure the plumbing was from the dark ages as it rattled and coughed into life in the mornings, nothing like those scenes in the James Bond movies. The bed, I am sure, came out of the Tsar's palace, it was so old. But when in places like Russia, you are not there to spend time in your room, you are out looking at the scenery and markets. So, the trendy hotel didn't matter.

I arrived in Sweden to find that they had also hired two males for the positions advertised. On arrival, we found the company in upheaval; they had just sacked their chief pilot and training captains and the company was in a mess. Many of the younger pilots were trying to have their say and it was very apparent that one or two of them didn't want a female captain. Not to worry, I thought, I shall see what is happening. We did the company induction course and having completed all the tests I was right to go once checked out to line and my instrument renewal for Sweden.

They took the two males first and I was told I was going to fly right seat— FO—I was one very unhappy female. The American who had joined the company at the same time as I, flew well but in the US, it is unusual for them to fly procedures, in other words, they rarely do a join overhead and then proceed to fly approach without direction from the tower. They are usually vectored straight on to final and fly the last sector of the approach. While his handling was excellent, his actual knowledge of how to do a procedural approach—an approach that was not controlled by someone telling him what heading to fly—was woeful. He was immediately designated to an FO position. Next, it was my turn. I took up my position in the right-hand seat thinking, *'I am looking for another position immediately; I didn't come here to be an FO, I am gone.'* As we lined up and took off, the new chief pilot said, "On reaching 500 feet just go to 1000 feet above ground level (AGL) and come back in to land." Stunned, I complied. As we landed, I was told to just taxi over there and shut down.

"Let's change seats, he said, I have never seen anyone so obviously in the wrong seat. You should be a captain and the FOs are just going to have to get used to having a female captain. You are the best handler I have ever seen." So, we swapped seats. He remarked that it was because I was so relaxed in and out of an aircraft that had made them think I was perhaps not captain material, not perhaps demanding enough, but I had always worked on the idea that a happy atmosphere doesn't have to mean less efficiency and soon they learnt that the smile on my face did not lessen my dedication, my efficiency or my adherence to my crew's welfare and safety. If I am safe, they are safe.

One FO challenged me into going into Gavle one night when the crosswind was 28 knots in Sweden; we were flying the same aircraft that I had been flying in Newcastle—the SD3-60.

I knew the aircraft had a crosswind maximum of 30 knots, so I was quite happy to land the aircraft. While an aircraft may be limited to 30 knots (that is quite often a demonstrated crosswind, meaning that was the strength the wind was blowing that day) its limit is actually when you run out of rudder. However, if you have an accident above the maximum that is in the flight manual, then there is no insurance. So, unless an emergency such as a fuel problem means you have to land, you stay within limits and so we had two knots to spare. I landed and it was as smooth and straight as any other landing. This young FO had been one of the ones who hadn't wanted a female captain. We had started the flight with him informing me that he had never had a woman captain before. I had just laughed and said sit back and enjoy the ride. Well after this landing, all problems were resolved, I was accepted.

I loved Sweden—a new learning curve, learning to deal with ice and snow, landing on snow braking factors. Dry snow, wet snow, de-icing types, all new. As Christmas approached one of the FOs told me the company was in trouble, as they had not received Christmas presents. I thought nothing of this, as I had never ever had a present off a boss. However, rumours started and I began to think there might be something to it. By now, the rumblings had become very numerous about the company going into liquidation, so again I started looking for another position. In the meantime, another Christmas was coming and I managed to get a weekend flight to Lulea. We picked some army personnel up in Ostersund and we were to fly them to Lulea, where on the Monday morning we were to do the trip in reverse. So, on closing the aircraft for the weekend we headed for the hotel. I had already booked a room at the ice hotel in Sweden. This is the original ice hotel and each year it is a different design. I caught the train, which was opposite the hotel the company had booked me, on reaching

Jukkasjarvi I caught a taxi to the ice hotel and had a great time. Here they don't put ice in your drink, here they serve you your drink in an ice glass. Next morning, I was off for a ride in a sled pulled by huskies.

Late afternoon saw me heading for the train back to Lulea. Monday saw me at the airport ready to depart back to Ostersund. I did see the Northern lights put on a full display one night and they danced around the airframe. Most evenings they just seemed to hang like green and magenta curtains. But this display was fantastic.

Another trip I did was on the tourist train (Inlandsbanan); here you just pull the cord when you want to swim in a lake or have afternoon tea and it took 12 hours to get from Hudiksvall to Gållivare. It leaves from Gothenburg and it is a slow train, it stops to let you pick strawberries or visit small villages. There was a stop as we entered the Arctic Circle and also at the mosquito museum, which, knowing the diseases that mosquitoes carry, I was not too keen to enter. However, it was amusing with lots of foliage and large photos of how people dress to safeguard themselves from mosquito bites. The photos showed people completely nude except for a pith helmet with mosquito netting falling from the brim of the helmet to the ground. Not a stitch on but no bites either, quite funny.

***

Another trip I did was on the Hurtigruten. I had been sent to Ostersund and had the weekend off so I decided to drive to Trondheim and catch the Hurtigruten up the coast to Boda. Killer whales swam alongside the boat. We saw the fjords and an old boat with an extremely funny sail; it looked like an old Viking-type vessel. On the way home, I had a sleeper and I slept nearly all the way, getting up early to disembark as soon as I could so I could jump in my car and return to Ostersund where I was rostered to fly. I was so lucky that I saw so much of Sweden and its neighbouring countries. I did a trip to Finland from there, only really long enough to step off the gangplank walk for 30 minutes and re-board, a bit disappointed as I would have liked to spend longer. The overnight trips across the Baltic Sea are just for drinkers.

I also had my car stolen as I had a small unit near the railway station; I woke up one morning and the car was gone. I asked my friends to ring the police on my behalf. They found it, but while it was in police custody it was stolen again. This time, they put the thief in the lockup.

***

Owing to the fact that I held an instructor rating, I was often asked to explain technicalities. I sometimes felt that the cockpit was more like a classroom. The number of times I said, "Wind does not affect Indicated Airspeed (IAS) it affects ground speed but not indicated airspeed!" I had to prove it every time by turning on the ice light.

100

Military pilots are trained differently than airline pilots as they have different objectives. I have met many military pilots who have transferred to airlines and are shocked to learn that they now must sit the exams that normal crew sit. I had learnt to listen; I took notice when told about ice build-up. In the short time I had been dealing with ice I had listened to my colleagues. It is so important getting the timing right as if you don't the problems will exacerbate. If you mention ice to Flight Service or traffic control you will be given priority. It is extremely dangerous and believe it or not I have experienced ice in the Sahara Desert.

Sweden has many very strict employment rules. The company I was working for seemed to be constantly trying to get rid of their own countrymen and employ outsiders like me because these rules did not apply to us. When I had time off with my broken wrist, I was told I would not be paid sick pay. My friends in Sweden rallied around and made sure I had translators and offered to help me with money but I was fine, but it was great to have such support.

The Swedes seemed to like their alcohol very much, the same as Australians. However, the difference is the fact that they do not drink to socialise, they drink to get legless (drunk). It was far different from my experiences in Oz where people will have one or two with a meal and that's it. In Sweden, I found that they rarely drank but when they did, it was full on and many were literally carried home from Christmas parties.

I did an overnight cruise across to Finland and came back the next day. Everyone seemed to go just to drink himself or herself silly. They danced, laughed, fell down, and went to bed somewhere around 0500 hours. They did not get off the boat in Finland but slept through the entire landing and got up in time to dock back in Sweden. Everyone had a great time.

I really like the Swedish people; they are warm, loving individuals who embrace life with gusto. However, considering how my colleagues were being treated, I realised this company was on the fast track to liquidation. So, I applied for another job. I believed the company I was working for was being mismanaged.

Sometimes it is more profitable to send a company down the drain providing you have got your assets tied up in another name, you should come out okay. But the people associated with you are left hurt and out of work. I have seen this many times throughout my life and can only say what goes around, comes around.

Not long after, I was offered a job with a Zurich company that had at one time held the Red Cross and United Nations contracts. At this time however, the contracts were held by a South African company. But I applied and was offered a position working out of Angola.

Chapter 26
Learning Some Life Lessons

The Swiss company had an induction course on joining their company as do all companies; you learn their dos and don'ts, living in places where there can be dangers you don't expect. One gentleman had been going in and out of Algeria for years, he lived a while there in a particular town and had gotten to know his neighbours. As he was getting supplies to put in his 4-wheel drive for this particular stay, he met, quite by chance, his neighbour's daughter who was attending University in Algers; she told him her 'sad' story. Apparently, the university had finished the semester and she had to wait some days for a bus home to her village, she didn't have enough to pay for accommodation and so he kindly offered to take her with him. It was an 8–10-hour drive but they would arrive before nightfall. He intended to leave early next morning, so it was agreed they would meet as soon as the sun was up so they could make good time. On delivering her safely to her family, they had him arrested and charged with rape. He honestly had not touched her as was later proved in court. It was just a chance to extort money. But he was thrown in jail awaiting trial, where other men raped him. Not only did he get a variety of sexually-transmitted diseases, he had a nervous breakdown and lost his job because if you're not mentally stable you can't hold a pilot's license. He also lost his wife and family as he became more and more depressed. This story was told to us at our induction. Do not think, "Sure, I will help." DO NOT TRUST, you are in a different culture and believe me they do not want us there. Not even when you are helping. Christ! Have the do-gooders got it wrong?! They hate us with a passion.

***

They also sent us to Toronto to be trained on an aircraft I already had 4000 hours on. They wanted their crew to operate the aircraft in a standard way. This works very well as I have flown for companies as an FO where we had to carry a notebook as to what each captain wanted. This is much more efficient, as all the crew know what to expect, it is also kinder to the aircraft. The major cost on any aircraft is maintenance as time before overhaul (TBO) is an important factor in operating Turbo props. In Toronto, I did the tourist thing—the CNN Tower with its glass floor, Niagara Falls. There were five of us on the course with another female who had been in 27 African countries and had many hours on type. She was a fount of knowledge on how to adapt, how to be safely independent, when to back away and when to press forward without getting your throat cut. It was decided we would partner one another in the simulator. Our training went well and while we were the only two females on the course and also in Angola, we never did become friends. Yes, we did things together, that old adage of circumstances making strange bedfellows and by that I am not intimating we were stamp lickers, (in other words, gay). We were just two females in a different environment. Of the three gentlemen on the course, two were just everyday men, polite and prepared to work hard. The other one was German and he made some very disparaging remarks about women in a male world etc. He was plain rude. You can take a swipe at me and I will let it go, come back for a second go and you are suddenly looking at death and destruction. I immediately came back at this brother of Adolph. I said, "Well, as far as I am concerned, men are only good for one thing and half of you aren't any good at that. I would rather have a vibrator, you know where it has been, you don't have to feed it and it doesn't talk back, PISS OFF." Dead silence; he was shocked. He hated me with a passion. No problem, we were both captains and so wouldn't have to fly together. However, one day we were short of FOs and crewing rang and asked if I would you mind flying with him. "Sure, I can do that," I said, "as for me, personalities stop at the cockpit door." However, he did not have the same philosophy as me. So, we never ever flew together.

I was given an in date for Angola. However, when dealing with consulates not everything goes smoothly.

I had to wait around London for a bit as the company sorted out my visa for Angola. Approximately six days before Christmas the company contacted me to say that they had a problem with my visa. They weren't able to send me to Angola until the new year. As luck would have it, I had two passports, the UK one which my company was holding to process the visa, and my good old Australian one. The 21st of December saw me boarding an aircraft for a week in Australia to spend Christmas with family. The flight was a real milk run, stopping everywhere. I had been calling my mother regularly since my dad had died and I could hear in her voice that she was lonely. She lived close to my sister and her family but she still missed Dad and the loneliness was obvious. The aircraft was late departing the UK, due to fog. I missed my connection in Frankfurt and was put on an aircraft to Singapore next morning instead of Tokyo. From there on to Brisbane and I finally arrived on the morning of the 25th. I must admit I knew the captain and many of the cabin crew so I was invited to the cockpit and given bottles of wine to take with me. I asked about customs. They just smiled and said all fixed. I don't know how but I was asked no questions regarding the extra alcohol.

This week amongst family showed me I didn't fit. Having arrived on Christmas morning and being told we were having Christmas lunch I said okay but I needed a nap as I had not seen a bed since the 21st. I sleep when the opportunity arrives as I may not get another chance for sometimes 24 hours. I know the regulators tend to police this these days.

My mother who had absolutely no idea of the sort of life I lived said you are NOT going to bed now it is daylight. So, I showered and made the best of it at lunch. I was just about brain dead, and I was ostracised for not appearing interested in their lives, only in aviation. No excuses were accepted and after a week full of snide remarks, I left so pleased to be going back to whatever adventure awaited me. I learnt from this—don't complain and never explain.

Chapter 27
Angola

Adventure did await, not only did you need a visa to enter Angola, you also needed one to leave. But the crews were fantastic and the flying was excellent. I shared a unit with two men and we had cars to get around. Luanda, the capital of Angola, had been such a beautiful city. There was an old wreck of a building that had been destroyed when the Portuguese left Angola. Designed by Monsieur Eiffel, it had been a palace made of wrought iron and glass; you could see how beautiful it had once been. While all the glass had been destroyed, the iron was still there.

Walking around, it was soon obvious that it was not really safe. It was the first place in the world I was mugged, and I also had an engine shot out. I flew with FOs who were Angolan and I decided the Angolan women are amongst the most beautiful in the world.

On arrival, I started line training and the European crews were great; we had Canadians, British, Portuguese, Australian, German and many other nationalities amongst the captains. The chief pilot was an Angolan, a good pilot and a lovely man. There were other Angolan captains but these were few and far between. Part of our job was to train up the FOs to be captains. Some were serious about learning and worked well with us but there was a hard-core group that thought 'The world owes me. My daddy's a general and I am just here for the girls and the money.' 'Kadonga' is the Angolan word for bribe. Bribery was rife, the FOs used to have their pockets bulging with kadonga. Just to get a seat, passengers would almost throw money at them.

We were sometimes hired out to local operators but other flights were private charter. One charter was to go to Sumbe and from there we were to fly to a grass strip and bring a patient out so he could be treated at a hospital. We were to track via Sumbe as before I joined the company another pilot had gone a little close to the known rebel areas and at his home, he had a souvenir that had been the tailpipe from his Otter. He had been hit by a SAM (Surface to Air Missile). I had seen this with my own eyes. We had definite 'no fly' areas. So off we went to pick up the patient and on collecting him we also collected his family, a very pregnant wife and a small child. The woman carried all their belongings on her head in an enormous bundle tied together in a sarong. On arrival back at Sumbe we had called ahead requesting that an ambulance be called to coincide with our arrival. On arrival there was no ambulance, as you must specify that it is for military. You do this regardless of whether it is actually a soldier and the military will pay. An ambulance will not attend unless sure of payment. As the young woman tried to get a taxi for her husband, no one would take her, as she had no funds. I gave her one hundred kwanzas, which is or was then the equivalent of one USD. That exchange rate is from an illegal moneychanger as the banks only gave about 750 kwanzas to the dollar. With that she was able to get a taxi and feed them for some time. The family goes with the patient to hospital as they provide the meals, toilet them, wash them and in general do the nursing. The doctors do the medical. Although, in this case, I believe there was little hope as gangrene has a stench about it.

When we landed at the grass strip, we had checked the windsock and landed in the direction shown. A few days later, an aircraft from another organisation landed at the same airstrip, only this time the wind was favouring the opposite end. They actually hit a landmine and the nose wheel was wiped out. There was a bit of shrapnel damage around the aircraft, but no one was injured. This was one of the reasons that when we used the unmade strips, we tried to take off when departing by using the same amount of runway we used when landing. There is a procedure that works well in order to accomplish this. I was just lucky, as I would have landed in that direction had the wind indication been for that direction. That could have been my aircraft that was damaged. I have been remarkably lucky in my career.

***

In Lubango there is a statue of Christ—the same as the one in Rio. I believe there is also one in Portugal and that the three Christs face one another with their arms open forming a triangle between the three countries Brazil, Angola and Portugal. I have seen all three of them, the third I saw in Lisboa the other week. I was speaking of this to a gentleman where I was staying and he informed me there are many 'Christ the Redeemers', out there so another myth busted.

There was also an Eiffel tower in the Congo but I have been told that it has been destroyed. I hope if Angola ever becomes a tourist mecca that the local authorities try to restore many of the lovely old buildings that inhabit the city. I came to learn that Angola is a very corrupt country and those of us who have lived there say that if you can survive in Angola, you can survive anywhere in Africa.

One of my colleagues tells the story of seeing a woman fall off the back of a truck in Lagos. The following car could not stop in time and ran over her, as did subsequent traffic. Five days later the council came out to remove the body but there was little left of her. I didn't see this happen but the colleague who told me has been to twenty-two African countries and I have only been to ten (so far).

Since the war has ended in Angola, they are trying to promote the country as a tourist destination and it is very beautiful. I understand that it is being cleaned up and to this end they will have to stop the locals defecating on the streets and along the Marginal (Illya), where everyone jogs or walks in the evening. It is always men you see doing this, never the women, but women sometimes urinate in front of you.

***

I never once saw a ticket purchased or had one handed to me by passengers boarding the aircraft. But the FO and security officer had their pockets bulging with kadonga. I only took an interest when their greed made it obvious that the aircraft would be overweight, or I could see someone who was sick, or looked like they needed help, and then I would say they are travelling with us. Often removing one of the ones who had paid a bribe to travel, trusting he got a refund from the FO.

Another time I was with a captain-in-training and as we arrived at Benguela, one of the traffic staff came out and talked to me. They had a woman they wanted to transport; she had been scalded. The captain-in-training had not been paid any kadonga to allow her to travel. "She cannot come." he said.

I said, "Yes, she can."

"Lower Safe is a consideration," was his argument.

"No, it's not, it is not a head injury, no loss of blood, we can travel at lower safe without problem." There is in aviation a Lower Safe Altitude (LSALT) or as the US call it minimum on route altitude (MORA). She was like a boiled tomato, skin splitting. The medic had put some dressings over her to protect her from infection. I must admit this captain was the only one who had ever challenged my decision in this sort of matter. But I am formidable when I decide someone needs my help.

Captain-in-training said, "I am captain, she is not travelling."

I said, "Well, I am pilot in command as I am the training captain and what I say, goes. Any more garbage from you and all those who should not be on this aircraft will be thrown off by me, do you understand me? She is fucking travelling. That is that!"

After I insisted that she was travelling with us, the traffic staff hurriedly put her on. The stretcher was tied down and secured and off we went. She was very brave and did not complain even though her skin was hanging off her in some areas where she had been badly scalded.

I hadn't flown with a burn patient before and the captain-in-training said that she had lung damage caused by the burns. I couldn't see how (as no actual fire) but as a precaution we flew at a lower level, the LSALT just in case, and kept in radio contact with stations along the track rather than going high and staying with the main air traffic control (ATC).

On arrival at Luanda the ambulance appeared and as she was loaded in the security man came up to thank me and asked if I knew what had happened to her. I said I didn't. He said that her husband was extremely jealous and had poured boiling water over her and that while she was writhing in pain, he threw on some more. He asked me what would I do in such a situation and if I were her, would I go back to such a husband? I immediately answered that yes, I would go back to him as soon as I was able. This caused him both surprise and glee; to think that a woman such as myself would accept such behaviour. However, this glee soon turned to shock when I said that the very first night, he was asleep I would pour boiling water all over his genitalia. This was cause for much consternation and I was treated with much more respect after this and also with caution. I was the sort of woman who could ruin a man's future.

One of my colleagues said they are very wary of you when you said what you would do. It has gone right around the airport. I just laughed.

***

One flight was down to Namibe, the airport was called Yuri Gargarin airport after the first man in space. My FO this day was one of the not so good ones George L. As we landed, he said, "You do the fuel and I will do the manifest, as you don't speak Portuguese."

"Okay," said I with fuelling completed and the water test completed. When checking for water in avtur, which is basically kerosene and a similar colour to water, you did a litmus test using litmus paper, which turns pink with the presence of water. I believe now there is a dye in avtur, making it a very pale-yellow gold. All done and ready to go. But there was no FO; I asked for him in the terminal and found that the traffic guys definitely spoke English. I had been scammed. "Where is he?" I got no answer. Seems he had a girlfriend in the town and had gone to get laid. I said, "GET HIM," and after a mad scramble, he finally arrived back, one hour and 30 minutes after he first left. Livid is the word that best describes me.

He came in full of excuses, saying, "Don't let the passenger know you are mad at me; they won't like flying and if you are cross it will make them nervous."

"Bullshit, you are dead meat, and I will feed you through a propeller, you fuckwit!"

"You can't talk to me like that. My Daddy is a general."

"That's okay. I have two propellers, one on each wing—one for you and one for Daddy." He quickly got the passengers on. We departed well over 90 minutes late. When we called in at Benguela I explained to the traffic guys what had happened and they provided a very quick turn around and we were on our way again. I had the feeling they already knew; the phones had been running hot. On arrival at Luanda the chief pilot just happened to be around and he congratulated me on giving George a serve. He said no one else is game because of his father. On the way home as we approached Luanda, George had pleaded with me not to tell anyone. His loss of face, balled out by a woman. He would suffer major embarrassment.

"Not my problem," was my answer, "you will not keep me or passengers waiting while you get your rocks off. NOT ON." Because I was not afraid of his stupid father or him, I told the chief pilot and he faced a disciplinary panel. He turned up to fly with me three weeks later a very chastened young man. Dad had intervened, that was the reason he still had a job. Anyone else would have been long gone. Even so, Daddy was told next time, nothing could save him.

***

My next flight with George was also eventful, only this time it wasn't George's fault, but it didn't stop him from trying to collect sexual favours from the young women passengers. We had come out of Benguela at maximum weight and had to call in at Port Ambion on the way home to deliver some of our passengers and their luggage. We also had to take on new passengers and some cargo, we had burnt fuel but even with fuel and passengers removed, the new luggage and cargo put us again at maximum weight. It was George's leg so he was pilot flying. At the end of the runway is a very large hill. As we climbed, we started a gentle turn to the right on climb to 8000 feet. We heard a weird noise like short bangs and then popping and I saw the left engine winding down. George immediately went to close down the wrong engine. I took over 'my aircraft' and then said, "The left engine has failed, closing left engine down, please check." As the procedure is that we both check that we are closing down the failed engine and the call goes, "Left engine failed, Left engine confirmed. Left engine propeller feathered, confirmed. Left engine feathered," and so the call goes till the vital action drill is completed. I did the vital action drill on my own as George was still not functioning. Then I called for the checklist to confirm that the shutdown procedure has been done correctly. The checklist actually confirms the initial actions but then goes on to tidy up such things as fuel pumps and other ancillary instruments and switches. We had heard passengers screaming.

By this time, I had the aircraft trimmed out, power on the live engine set. Fuel pumps off, on dead engine. We were monitoring and reassessing our situation. I sent George with what little water we had on the aircraft down to the passengers and asked him to talk to them, give them water and to tell them this is what we are trained for and that they were to stay calm. If they had any questions they could ask and we would answer honestly, at that moment I had decided to continue to Luanda. We had called Flight Service and told them, we were continuing to Luanda, on one engine. This was against George's wishes, he wanted to return to Port Ambion. These decisions are made with discussion between the two pilots as we put our reasons for our decision. My decision was to continue to Luanda, as at Port Ambion when the airport was not in use, goats, pigs and cattle roamed free across the runway and they only use to clear it when a flight was due to land. As soon as the flight departed all the animals were once more let loose. We had also heard that the rebels had control of some of the local areas. I knew from colleagues that my passengers would be slaughtered along with my FO and I would be taken hostage for ransom. Our company was good and paid ransoms. Two of my colleagues had been taken hostage and it is an unpleasant experience. I, as a female, may not be treated as well. I knew there was a military airport about 50 nautical miles away. When we had given our call to Flight Service a company aircraft called and said, "We hear that airport is in rebel hands, if you can make 50 nautical miles then you can make 100." This confirmed my decision to make for Luanda. Flight Service started hassling for revised estimated time of arrival (ETA) and passenger names. George who by this time had thumb in bum and brain in idle couldn't work out a revised ETA. At this, I cut in and told them our revised ETA and that they were to go away. They could get our manifest from Port Ambion I was too busy to muck around with an engine out and FO who was more hindrance than help. I sent him down the back again, no questions from anybody, they were just pleased to be still airborne.

He came back this time and said, "It is my leg, I want to fly."

"Okay, your aircraft," I said, handing over.

He took over control and immediately said it was not in trim. I said, "It is trimmed to its limit because we need power, with maximum weight and one engine. I have 50 torque on the right engine so you need a little extra pressure on the rudder."

Immediately, he said, "I can't hold pressure for 100 miles."

"Well, you can reduce power but I feel it needs what I have set."

"I am not flying the aircraft like that, it is yours." I took over again and at this time I was handling the aircraft plus radio as he sat there and looked good in his uniform.

On arrival at Luanda, the tower told me to go into the hold. I said, "No, we still have an engine out."

"Sorry, I forgot, you have been so calm, we will clear you to land but you will have to land 05. That is the reciprocal of runway 23, which was the duty runway."

When we touched down the passengers broke into cheers and clapping while the tower said, "expedite clearing runway". I did the best I could and taxied to our parking. The engineers were all over the aircraft in moments. As they dropped the cowl on the left engine it was obvious the damage was catastrophic, there were small pieces of lead in the hot section. At first, we thought the aircraft might have had a counterfeit part. Our engineers were excellent and maintenance was good but this aircraft was fairly new to our line. Then we spotted holes in the cowl underneath the engine. George, god bless his cotton socks, true to form was going around the passengers as they stood and talked about still being alive. George was singling out the younger pretty women suggesting he had saved their lives and wanted a phone number so he could arrange to come round and collect. He was a randy little bastard. The only thing he said to me was, "I learnt something today, Captain."

"What was that?" I said. "To always fly your aircraft; you, never, for one minute, stopped flying, you are the reason we made this. It is over 100 miles from where we had the failure, Captain. You did radio and kept our fuel in balance."

"Yes, Captain, I have learnt." I seriously don't know if he ever did.

My engine failure incident was reported in the local newspaper as 'Old lady saves aircraft'. I was approaching 60 and you cannot fly in Angola over sixty, crazy when it is more dangerous to walk due to landmines.

On days off, we used to go some miles out of Luanda to a market, I have a beautiful little table from there with three legs, which are all made from one piece of wood and are all entwined. Also, some rather nice pieces of solid wood, hippopotamus, gazelle, rhinoceros, some very clever carving and woodwork.

I also became a member of Hash House Harriers but due to my intermittent lifestyle never got a Hash name. Hash is usually for younger runners but this group in Angola had an older group that were just walkers.

What a fun organisation. I met and made friends from many nationalities. We used to go out into the country in a group and see things we could never see if we were alone because it would not be safe. We would sometimes go through some of the settlements with their small markets and I learnt to haggle and broker deals on all sorts of things.

I have belonged to the Hash House Harriers in three countries, it was such good fun in the Hash circle afterwards when we had barbeques and drinks, it was always a laugh. I was in Angola when 9/11 happened and some of my Hash friends were involved with the US embassy. It was through Hash that I met the women who helped a priest run a school for the local homeless kids.

This priest ran this school as he had himself been a homeless child and had been taken under the wing of three American soldiers who were in Africa during the Second World War. When the War finished, they decided that they would pay for this young man to go to the US for an education. He became a priest but was unable to stay in the US and decided he should return home. But at that time Angola was in turmoil. The Portuguese were decolonising Angola and as they departed, they committed gross acts of destruction. They poured cement down toilets and wrecked infrastructure. As the sovereign state of Angola was born, having gained its independence in 1975, its politics were changed forever. So instead this young priest went to Portugal. He didn't stay long and soon realised he wouldn't fulfil his ambition to be of assistance to 'God' and he quickly moved back to Angola where he wished to minister to a flock. The transition he imagined, had not taken place and on his return, he was faced with almost insurmountable turmoil. He started taking care of some young homeless children, over the years this group of children has grown to four thousand.

The women from the embassies had learnt of his work over the years and had started to help. Each day they provided one decent meal for the children. Some of these women had been teachers and so they started teaching classes in English and Math. The small community of children in the city of Luanda grew but the only thing the Angolan Government did for the priest and his growing flock was to provide shipping containers in which to house, educate and feed them. Angola is rich in oil and diamonds but yet all the government gave was a few lousy shipping containers.

Santos (the president) would go for a holiday to Argentina where he would tip the concierge of his hotel 3000 USD, but take no responsibility for his own

111

people. There was a young man at the local supermarket who had lost both legs, blown off by landmines, during the civil war. He wore his thongs on his hands to get around. He used to sit outside the supermarket begging. There was an older man at Benguela airport. He had both arms and legs blown off. He was just a torso and head.

No wonder when he was departing in his private jet, they closed the airport for one hour before and after his departure or arrival. The civil war that has allowed so many land mines to be put anywhere and everywhere was simply between two men—one owned the oil and the other owned the diamonds. Both wanted what the other had. You have all heard of blood diamonds, well this is where all that started. We know Rwanda has had problems in this area also. Once Swambi (Santos's rival) was killed the war was over.

At Hash, we mixed with the people of the consulates and international journalists, and while I cannot supply proof, politics was the major discussion during our walks. What is written here is a result of those walks. It was also told that the US was in bed with Santos while the CIA was in bed with Swambi, so it didn't matter who won, the yanks had their feet in the door. The world's policeman? What garbage! What is good for the US is good for the US, bugger the rest of the world.

The reasons for closing the airport to normal flight traffic when Santos was going somewhere, was to prevent rebels setting up with 'SAMS' the hour after departure, in case the aircraft had to return.

However, this caused havoc for local operators having filed flight plans. All of a sudden, the departure time was irrelevant, as president Santos was departing. Or you were returning and listened to the airport information (ATIS) and you would be informed that the airport was closing at such and such a time. If we could not land by that time, we were told not to enter the Control Area. Therefore, they removed our destination airport; we were supposed to just hang there, with literally nowhere to go. All of a sudden, our arrival times were earlier. Yes, we lied. What are we supposed to do? Crash burn and die for some despot? We lied. There was a female controller in the tower who was brilliant, only one I have ever met who rivalled the UK guys for preciseness and responsibility. If she was in the tower, we knew we would be all right. She would let us in. We would all get home.

Angola is a beautiful country and its landscape is filled with mesas (flat-topped mountains). Flying here was wonderful, although like all countries it has weather phenomena that makes one wonder what the hell, we are doing up there in an approaching tempest.

On one occasion, while a major storm went through, we were stacked over the navigation aid, when one of the aircraft, A Hercules (C170), declared an emergency; it was running on vapours so they were cleared to land. I am not sure what happened but apparently the aircraft broke into three on landing.

The Russians were in Angola and would quite often pass through your level ignoring all efforts to remain clear of traffic. It is said they turned up to fly half tanked as you had to be drunk to fly their dilapidated aircraft. I have since come to respect the Russian aviation scene because while what they fly may not be pretty, and the engineer needs to be a tractor mechanic, they build a bloody strong aircraft. I have seen them operate in many countries throughout the world and those aircraft carry the most enormous loads. I cannot believe they do a weight and balance. At Bujumbura in Burundi I saw one take the length of the runway to get airborne and even then, they only just cleared the trees at the end of the runway, so overloaded were they. Gaining altitude as they flew the length of Lake Tanganyika, the only way they could have got another thing in that aircraft would have been with KY Jelly.

I had set myself a limit for daily giving. You would pull up at a corner checking for traffic with beggars everywhere. If you threw money out of the window of the car, what appeared to be missing arms and legs, suddenly appear out of sleeves and trouser legs while they fought for what they could get. It quickly became apparent that donations should only be given to the women, as they put it to good use feeding their children and buying necessities. The men could be seen pissing it up against a tree a few hours later, having purchased beer. Africa runs on the backs of its women. As do most countries. But at least in the more advanced countries women are slowly being recognised for their value.

***

Between our accommodation and the airport there was an area we called Dead Man's Hill. It was an area where the locals would throw themselves in front of the car and then try to hold us to ransom for their 'injuries'. As we traversed this area, we would be extremely careful and aware. One of our colleagues—a Norwegian gentleman—refused to drive and the rest of us took it in turns. Yes, he wanted the money paid for flying in this country but would not take his turn at driving. Another colleague had been driving home when the man who threw himself in front of the car misjudged and ended up under the wheels and died. The police were called and the driver was taken to jail. This is where it is so important that the company you are working for is a good company. The European company that employed us believed that justice would run its normal course, while the Angolan company that leased us from the European company immediately provided a guard 24 hours a day to protect the pilot. They were employed to stay with him until trial. He was given a bail hearing, and the story goes a 10,000 USD bribe was paid to allow him out on bail, more money was paid and he was out of the country. There was money for the visa to leave and so it went. I know the UK Consulate has its own jail cell in the cellar of the consulate. I had been invited for supper, and was given a tour. I am sure other consulates have similar set-ups. However, it is better to use the local jail as if someone escaped from the custody of an embassy, great embarrassment would be incurred.

Then on getting to the airport you had to go through immigration and here the officers would take you into a little cubicle and asked for your passport and this they would hold to ransom, suggesting you pay them. This was normal, all of us had large amounts of cash on leaving Angola as we would be given a food allowance, which was rather nice and we considered it danger money. But the theory was that the company didn't want us cooking as we were already under stress. However, going out to dinner was stressful. So, this man in passing through immigration, got the full treatment even though the company had already paid people off.

When I went through immigration, I used to write down the number of every note in my possession and tell them I had faxed a copy to my company. I was to be met by a company representative to see if I still had all the money. If I didn't, questions would be asked. This worked and I was always allowed through with this ruse.

Stupidly the European company tried to send the pilot involved in the fatal accident back in for another tour of duty. The Angolan company again stepped in and he never made it through immigration, they had a ticket out on same flight he had just entered the country on.

***

One day, I was just going for a walk along the Illya as I made my way through the back streets to this area, two 12-year olds accosted me. Their intention was to rob me. One tried to pull my watch off as another went for my backpack, this brought them within my reach and as I gave them a clip around the ears and a kick up the arse, one pulled a knife. I wish I could say I had the equivalent of Crocodile Dundee's knife in the movie with the comment, "Ya call that a knife?" I was unarmed and it looked like it was turning serious when along came a Tamata (means trouble and given that name by the expats). But here a Tamata is a people-carrying vehicle, usually blue, the one I travelled in you could see the road through the holes in the floor. The lads took off as the driver yelled at them, I continued on my way, smiling, and waving to thank the driver.

Another day, my female colleague (Sara), and I were going to the internet café. Anytime we went out we were supposed to carry a two-way radio, as we walked up the hill to the café, I was lagging behind just a little when I saw two black hands and arms grab for the antenna on Sara's radio. I immediately locked my hands together using my arms to break his hold on the antenna and it was really the start of a large altercation. I was thrown into the bushes by the other one of the two. I jumped up extracting myself from the bushes, and bleeding a little from the prickles. I was straight back into the fray. I was just about to hit the one attacking Sara, who by this time was on the bonnet of a car, her arms and legs moving like pistons, but also protecting the radio, when some security guards from a local bank came running with batons ready for business. The muggers took off, with me chasing them down the street yelling "Bastardos!" while Sara, the guards and general populace were yelling for me to stop. They used to steal our radios and then call the company on the company frequency and hold them to ransom. Sara and I dusted ourselves off and went for coffee after our little fisticuffs. I laughed as I thought of my mother being shocked at me, nearly 60 and scrapping in the streets of Angola. At no time did it occur to us to call the police. Somehow, they would have found some way to make it our fault and we would have ended up paying.

On arrival back at my apartment one of my male colleagues was sitting there when he noticed my dishevelled state. He started lecturing me about us girls going out. I said, "Go-away, when you got mugged they got everything—camera, wallet, ID, Passport—the fucking lot. Sara and I fought and they got fuck all so don't lecture me."

One day, I arrived at work and was told we were transporting prisoners. There were four very raggy-baggy men waiting on board. I looked at the four men inhabiting the rear of the aircraft and asked which ones were the prisoners. I was told that they were the ones who didn't have laces in their boots. On closer inspection, two of the men had their boots on with the laces removed. This was supposed to stop them from running away, because the boots were too loose for running.

One day, we arrived at a country airstrip to find a large group of very young lads, around twelve, all standing in rows. They had been conscripted from a local village. We were told they were being recruited for the army and within weeks would be in charge of AK47s. Unbelievable, but that is the reason these young men begging at the supermarkets had no limbs, all for two men who wanted what the other one had. CRIMINAL.

One of my gripes in working for this Swiss company was that I had been lied to. When I applied, I told them my age and wanted to work until at least 65. Not a problem I was told, while you can pass your medical. I have since been told that this is a Swiss trait to tell you what you want to hear as long as it gets them what they want. Having been informed that my next tour of duty would be my last, as I was to turn 60 and was to wait for a vacancy in either Chad or Cameroon, I was also told during this stand down time that I would not be paid. So, I decided to go to South Africa and visit a safari park. Sara had informed me there was a company there looking for high time Otter pilots. I hired a car with the intention of heading to Pilanesberg, which I thought would take me through Lanseria where the company Sara had told me about was located. I wanted to drop my CV off at this company. I arrived at Lanseria and found the company. As I walked through the hanger I was told where I could find the operations department and crewing. So, I went as directed, found the office and started talking to the two ladies on duty. I was told that they had nothing at that time but yes, they would have a look at my CV and off I went. On arrival at Pilanesberg I was just getting acquainted and looking for accommodation when my phone rang and it was the lady from Lanseria. Could I go to Burundi tomorrow? I was to go through Nairobi and overnight at the Safari Club where I would have a suite of rooms. "WOW!" I said, "Well, I am at Pilanesberg. Yes, I can drive back to Jo' burg now."

"We will wait at the office for you but we would like to send you to Burundi for eight weeks."

"Sorry, no can do. I am just on break from my job in Angola. I have one more tour of duty there and then I am available permanently."

"Okay, that will get us out of a hole. We will get your tickets and book your hotel in Nairobi. Can you come back now?"

"On my way."

So, having just arrived and removed my case from my boot I put it back and headed back down to Lanseria where the two ladies from the office were waiting for me. Having picked up my tickets and rung the hotel I had used the previous night for a room, I was set to go to Burundi early next morning. This little country is surrounded by five other countries and is landlocked. Bujumbura, the capital of Burundi sits on the shore of Lake Tanganyika. However, first stop was Nairobi and the Safari Club. What a fantastic hotel! Next morning, on my way to Burundi, Greg (real name) my FO was to show me the ropes and introduce me to the other crew. He was a very happy young man and a real delight both in the cockpit and just to be with. When he walked into a room it was like the sun just got up. All smiles and seemed genuinely happy, loved flying and took great care of the 'old lady'. Apparently the two ladies in Lanseria when describing me told him I was an old lady. We were in the 'Red Cross' house. The company had two crew houses in Burundi and I was put on the Red Cross contract. One morning very early the phone rang and Greg knocked on my door. He said that as we left today, we were to take all our belongings with us. They are finding somewhere else for us to stay tonight. So, we went off to work not knowing where we would be that evening. It seems that they had intelligence that rebels were entering the town down a dry riverbed that ran past the back of the house.

I finished the three weeks and came back to South Africa having had a new experience and thoroughly enjoying myself. On arrival back at Lanseria where I went to see them to receive my pay and I had paperwork to hand in. On arrival I was told the chief pilot wanted to see me. He welcomed me to his office and said, "I believe you work for us."

I just grinned and said, "Well, I have for 3 weeks."

"How would you like it to be permanent—when can you start?"

I said, "Mid-November, I am going to Nepal to see Mt Everest in November but after that I can start."

"Could we expect you here on the 20th for an induction course?" And so once again I was employed. In the meantime, I caught my flight back to Angola and finished my tour of duty. We were supposed to stay eight weeks. We worked eight in, four out, but while I was in country something went wrong with one of the guys due to come in and I was asked to stay extra weeks. Not a problem, there was still a couple weeks to my 60th birthday. During these extra weeks I realised why we worked such a roster, as by the time it came to leave, I was well and truly past my use by date. The stress you felt when flying, while manageable over eight weeks, by twelve weeks was making me ratty. I was very pleased to leave at the end of the extended tour. Good colleagues, good lifestyle when not flying, at the beach or markets, but the constant aggression was tiring. Being shot at if you went a little close to no-fly zones, the begging in the streets, constantly having to be aware of what was happening around you, who was near you. Walking along the Illya one day a young man ran past me, he was going flat out when I heard a voice call out to stop. No response from the fleeing felon. Next I heard an AK47 ratchet up, they make a noise as they get ready to fire. The young man stopped in his tracks and surrendered.

I told the company, as much as I enjoyed working for them, I had been offered a position with a South African company as I had no wish to wait around waiting for a placement in either Chad or Cameroon.

***

Chapter 28
Nepal and Burundi

Off I went for my holiday in Nepal. It was a tour through an English company. I usually don't do tours, but a girl friend had approached me and asked if I would go with her as the tour company would only do the tour if there were four people on it. So, I said yes and very early November saw me heading to Nepal. Unfortunately, my friend dropped out at the last moment due to the breakout of hostilities in Afghanistan. Very late in day to cancel but the tour company seeing the guides were already there and were local Nepalese people, decided to continue with the tour. I really hate tours. I like to wander, but this was fantastic. We went white water rafting, which was nothing like the Specke Falls in Uganda at the head of the Nile, something I was to do later. We went to Tiger Lodge where you go looking for tigers within a refuge. We never found any; I am pleased to report. They did tell us what to do if we saw one and there were tiger paw prints in the earth, but it's possible someone was walking around with a tiger paw on a stick, as I never seemed to see four together. But it was a great break and I saw Mount Everest. When we were white water rafting, we spent a night in a very glamorous camp on the edge of the river. Shower, campfire—the works, it was very well done, I had a really wonderful time.

On one of my walks I met a little boy about four, who told me his name was Sue. Shades of Johnny Cash, I think that little boy would have become most proficient at taking care of himself. The temples, food and people were just wonderful.

Straight back to Burundi, here again it was eight weeks in country and four weeks out. On arriving I met an older South African gentleman who informed me he was the reason I was hired. It seemed he was due to go in to do a tour of duty when it was discovered his medical had lapsed. Most companies inform you when your medical is due. But some don't and he had forgotten and with no warning from the company he could not fly, hence the frantic phone call when I was at Pilanesberg.

The other thing I learnt was that in the house they had moved us from on the first tour, the new occupant had been macheted to death. One of the other aid agencies had put someone quite senior in for his visit to Burundi to oversee his organisation's endeavours. As he sat out on the step this night having a cigarette the rebels who came into town by the dry riverbed at the rear of the house, killed him with a machete. Smoking definitely kills, but not usually in this manner.

Most organisations have their own intelligence in these areas but some are better than others.

While in Burundi, we spent quite a lot of time socialising with the young American troops who were billeted in the house directly behind what we pilots called the 'United Nations (UN) house'. They had even broken-down part of the fence separating the two houses to give greater access. This gave my young South African colleagues a false sense of protection as they felt their 'friends', and I use that term loosely, would help if we at any time came under attack. Well we did come under attack and they didn't come to our rescue. I didn't expect them too as I have worked with Americans before. In their own country they are lovely, hospitable people but their military think they are better than they are. As we Aussies would say, "Legends in their own minds."

But because we went out into the countryside, we saw things they didn't. I find that the Americans are never in any country unless there is something of interest in that country for them. They are not there for good deeds; they are there for American advantage.

So, we, who were out there every day, being shot at and taking risks were treated as special friends, but only if they could get information. The head of the embassy security, which in most cases is actually military intelligence, always came around with the 'troops'. This man was so disparaging of his colleagues I was disgusted.

He stated, "Dog faces! Those stupid bastards don't have a brain between them, tell them to jump out of an aircraft at 10,000 feet and they would without a parachute if you told them they would be okay."

I must admit that conversation with many of the young men indicated that they did not have a large repertoire of anecdotes.

One constantly said of himself, "I am a real tart; I have had more than fifty women." Another's entire conversation consisted of the word, 'Fuck.' I am sure that was all he ever said.

So, perhaps the head of security was right that maybe they were pretty dumb. The other military guys we hung out with were the South African Army who were actually camped on Bujumbura Airport, which is why on more than one occasion we would be coming back to base and find ourselves under mortar fire.

These guys loved good food and would often call in to see what I was cooking the weekend, as our houseboys took the weekends off and I enjoyed cooking for a group. My mushroom soup was always a hit.

I upset the head of embassy security one day when we argued about 9/11.

I said, "I have worked in and out of different embassies for a long time and have listened to the goings on, there were no weapons of mass destruction."

He was cross and argued, "You will see, the UK is about to become the 51st state of the USA."

"No way."

The conversation got hostile.

He threatened, "If you do anything to my career or cause me any damage in any way, I will make sure you disappear, I will waste you."

I observed, "Great, you are going to kill an Australian, who is working for the Red Cross and the UN, someone who is unarmed. Good luck explaining that, I could hardly be called collateral damage."

Present during this exchange was a man from the embassy security of Kigali (Rwanda) and he was almost apoplectic trying to shut him up. He kept interjecting, "That's true, she is correct. He (Saddam Hussein) did get the weapons from us during the Iran problem."

"No, they had been dispersed with," I argued.

He (the American from Kigali) obviously agreed with me as he said, "Yes, Hussein used those against Iran."

The security man was really trying to make the American shut up after his threat.

The American (local to Burundi) visited the UN house, the pilot's quarters the next evening, on a night that he usually didn't visit. He was very friendly and sat and talked to the other pilots in general. When I left the room, he followed me to the kitchen.

He started, "Just as well you can take a joke and know when I was joshing."

He went on and on about how I had a sense of humour, a great sense of humour and there were no hard feelings. Military intelligence—what an oxymoron! The last part is correct anyway, he was a moron with little intelligence.

However, to give him his due, one of the Red Cross workers said how he had helped save his life when they were in Beirut. I never got to know the full story but from what I understood, he helped the Red Cross worker by dragging him across some rubble and into a safe area. I was surprised to hear this as to my knowledge when their staff is threatened, the Red Cross get their people out very quickly.

My comment was succinct, "We both know you weren't joking but at least now I figure I am safe because your colleague has obviously had a word in your ear. Let's just keep things polite and keep out of one another's way in future."

I worked for this company for some time and even though it didn't always pay I thoroughly enjoyed the people. It was fun and friendly and I felt appreciated. They really seemed to care, at least Sharon, who hired me, did. Sharon is one of those rare exceptions in life who, when things are going wrong, will do her best to solve the problem and seek advice from those who should know. But if for some reason or another she can't get an answer, she will make a decision and stand by it, taking the lumps herself and not hanging her crew out to dry. I don't know if this lady knew how highly she was thought of.

While working on these contracts, we were quite often in danger and just going to the gym could be dangerous. The locals would aim their cars at us and try to run us down. It got so bad that I carried a rock to aim at their windscreens. Our houses were shot up. They liked having foreigners around for the financial resources and the help of NGOs but in their heart of hearts they did not want us in their countries.

We had guns pointed directly at us. I laugh when I have some person in Australia threaten me. Our local airport CEO is an example of someone whose threats are such a joke, he is always saying he is going to report me for something or other and I just think, "Woopdidoo! I tremble in my shoes." These people have no idea of the lifestyle that I, and people like me, have lived and worked in. I learnt not to kiss arse as people lose respect for you and without respect you have nothing.

We heard stories of passengers at one airstrip that were all slaughtered. Nurses would go to the local hardware store to get a key cut and the shopkeeper would cut a second key and auction it off and the nurse would be raped by a group of locals. The only way to get keys cut was to send a man along with a local man who worked for the organisation.

I will say this for the Red Cross, once their people were hurt, they moved everyone else out. Also, they started housing the ladies together with guards posted.

In Angola, my flat overlooked what had been the UNHCR building. They had departed when there was unrest and had left all of their cars there to rot, there must have been thirty of them, all four-wheel drives and all expensive. That is one of the reasons I do not give/ donate to these organisations. The waste is criminal.

This is where I saw Africa at its worst. We had a houseman who looked after us—did our washing (I always washed my own underwear as everything was hand washed), cleaned our rooms and was an excellent cook. Also, there were two security guards at the UN house and at the Red Cross house we had a security guard plus a houseboy. The UN house had three pilots and an engineer. While the Red Cross house just had the two pilots, captain and FO. We had cars that we would drive to the airport. At the airport was a contingent of the South African Army. They were there to help train the Burundi Army. The Hutus and Tutsi spoke the same language and had the same religion and the same culture. They had lived peacefully together for years until the differences between their tribes were emphasised by the European invaders, the Germans and the Belgians. In Burundi the Tutsis were in the minority but managed to maintain control of the military and so slaughter occurred. This problem had been going on since 1959 and was still going in 1994. The military purchased machetes from China for 10 cents, I believe because they were cheaper than bullets. So, our white faces were not welcome.

It was here that I first learned to like the sound of gunfire, we worked on the idea if we could hear gunfire, they were letting off steam, if we couldn't we were worried that they were planning an attack and we were not safe. It was great flying but one day I was with Greg and we had landed at Muyinga. This airfield is approximately five kilometres from the border of Burundi and Rwanda and we always only closed down one engine. As we loaded and unloaded, Greg was out there supervising and with doors closed we tried to start the left engine, but it wouldn't start. We did our usual checks but no, it was kaput, absolutely nothing. So, we put out a call to company and said we needed an engineer. We were then informed that the rebels from Rwanda were crossing the border. We took the passengers off and closed down the right engine, as we were going nowhere. We managed to borrow a ladder and with the help of the engineer on the HF, we were told to remove igniters from the live engine. Greg was up there top of ladder checking each engine, but we couldn't remove an igniter from the right engine and put it in the left engine in order to get a start. As each engine has two igniters or glow plugs an aircraft is built with both engines having the same type of system. But this was an old aircraft which had, had an engine replaced and while one side had igniters the other had glow plugs. We were, to put it bluntly, fucked.

We heard from base that Dean, our engineer, had boarded the UN aircraft and he was coming to us with igniters. He was knowingly flying into an area where the possibility of, at best, being taken prisoner was a very real threat along with just plain being murdered. The UN aircraft approached, but did not close down any engines as we were used to being near propellers. He came out with a ladder and toolbox (this toolbox has its own story) in which he had put the igniters; we had let down the bottom cowl and had removed the top. Greg helped him re-cowl and having replaced the failed parts, we put on those passengers who had returned to the airport with us and we were gone.

Dean's toolbox, of which he was so proud, came to a sad end. At Bujumbura, Dean used a tractor for towing aircraft and by clambering up on the tractor he could gain access to the wings etc. He was so engrossed this day in fixing a problem, along with the roar of other engines starting and taking off, he didn't notice his toolbox had fallen off the tractor and as he finished up the job he ran over his toolbox with the tractor. He also did similar to an aircraft part which he had to panel beat out. He did such a good job no one ever noticed.

On my next time out, I was to return to Australia to renew ratings and I also renewed my instructor rating. I had borrowed a young instructor to sit in the left seat as I needed to do a little bit of work in the right seat. I fly a very tight circuit and often remark to students that I am not carrying a packed lunch as I am not doing a navigation exercise. The circuit is supposed to be within an area that if your engine failed, you could glide back to the airport. So, I was flying my usual tight circuit when she mentioned I could go a little further afield. I resolutely stuck to my standard circuit. Some years later, I ran into this instructor again. She greeted me with, "I now know why you do tight circuits."

"You know, those tight circuits of yours scared me," she continued, "I have been out too," and she named a couple of really normal countries, stating that it scared the shit out of her, being in close proximity to various obstacles.

I just laughed and said, "That is not my reason. At some places I have been, the airport is close to the border and if you infringe on their airspace they will and do shoot you down. That is why I do a tight circuit. No other reason, except in a single engine I would like to be able to make the airport, if not a runway."

Yes, we were in turboprop twins, but believe me, there is no incentive like getting shot at to keep the circuit tight. There is one airport/landing strip in PNG when the Indonesian air force chased you and fired at you even though that strip is approximately 10 nm from the border, they are aggressive. Yes, I have landed there—it's a great barramundi fishing spot.

Back to Burundi, this time on the UN contract, I was told to attend their offices before I was to fly the next day. We were flying for the World Food Program here. But all new pilots to the contract were hauled in, for advice on how to stay safe. One piece of paper detailed what to do if you are in a crowd that someone had just thrown a grenade into.

We did the same strips as the Red Cross aircraft but in the UN aircraft we carried NGOs. These people went to teach methods of agriculture. Burundi is, or perhaps I should say was, one of the most populated countries in the world because of small land mass and large population, so they use every piece of land available to grow crops. Even the roundabouts were full of plants to eat. The main local transport was bicycles and they would carry the most enormous loads on their bikes.

Again, there was a Hash House Harriers contingent and the UN house back neighbour were the US Consulate's security contingent. I used to tell the pilots, "Keep your mouth shut because if push comes to shove, they will throw us to the wolves." That did happen one September 16th. I spent five hours in the downstairs toilet as the rebels shot up the house. The other pilots were with me. The toilet was the only room in the house without windows and it had double brick walls, which kept us safe. Our security had fled for their lives and rightly so. They were not armed, basically they were gardeners who also stayed to open the gates as we arrived and left. On another tour of duty, I told the refueller off, he drove in under the wing of the Otter at speed and nearly hit the propeller. I got reported and was accused of racism.

I just laughed and said, "I don't care what colour he is. He could be black, white, green, pink, yellow, any flaming colour, what he did was stupid." So, I got quite a negative report to the company. However, next tour the refueller did the same thing and this time he misjudged and did hit the prop and took it out of feather. That cost 2.5 million to fix. Again, I just smiled and said 'told you so'. No one else had been game to complain, none of the pilots. Yes, they all talked about it, but due to being accused of racism if we did complain they kept quiet. If it had been a white guy, they would have sacked him. But no, the old cry stopped common sense. My next report was brilliant, as they learnt I didn't talk or growl just for the sake of it. When I said something, I meant it. Had they listened they would have saved themselves a lot of money. He would have kept his job, but no. I was ignored, labelled a racist and it cost them 2.5 million.

***

One night we went out to dinner and I got the job of talking to the guys about sex. I don't know if it is true but back then one of the Red Cross ladies told me that AIDS was called the Red Cross disease and that many of the men in the Red Cross ended up with it. The saying was 'try black, never come back'. Black velvet, it was called amongst the Red Cross girls. These women are truly remarkable—they would enter the prisons, treat the inmates, and sometimes provide counselling, helping in any way they could. One of their male colleagues had a nervous breakdown on board and when we returned to Bujumbura this day, he never got off the aircraft, he just sat there huddled in his seat. They wanted us to fly very high and then circle down. Our theory was that circling down made us an easy target and we used to fly at not LSALT but at LBSALT (Lower Bullet Safe Altitude). As we approached, we came down to tree top height and dropped into the airport at Rygui—our quickest turnaround there was 1 minute 30 seconds. As we landed, the rebels were at the end of the runway with AK47s. The FO ran down the back while I was still taxiing and closing down the left engine, we always kept the right one going. The agent pulled luggage out, put luggage on and the FO got the passengers on and off. While he was closing the backdoor and running back to his seat, I was taxiing and we took off straight into their direction. Because of their gear, they were not as fast as they might have been and a runway, even a dirt strip, is usually at least a kilometre long. The Otter will operate in much less and I have used a strip in Vanuatu that was 300 metres long. You have reverse for landing and don't land into the strip, your aiming point is the near end. Then reverse, just before touchdown, you literally fall out of the air inches off the runway. Taking off, you use a short field procedure and most of us could get it off the ground in approximately 90 meters. Full power feet on brakes, control column in tummy and two stages of flaps and she unsticks at maximum weight at 45 knots, you then fly level around 20 feet off the ground and stay in ground effect (a bubble of lift forms around the wing, its height approximately the length of the wing span and acts as a cushion) as speed builds, you retract flap slowly, one stage at a time and fly away normally. Brilliant aircraft.

Rygui had an orphanage run by an Irish woman named Pat. I never met her, but she was a legend with the Red Cross nurses. She founded the orphanage and supported these children. Once a year she heads to the US and other countries and raises funds by speaking and telling stories. Every time any of us held a social event, be it pilots, Red Cross or consulates there was always an entry fee— a piece of clothing, T shirts, sandals, trousers—we would throw them on the aircraft to help her at least clothe the kids in the orphanage. On Sundays, a few kids would come to our gate and we would feed them but nothing on her scale. Back to my passenger who wouldn't disembark, this man was extremely nervous. He was a negotiator and he would sit at a table with men who had guns, machetes, knives, grenades and very violent personalities. He would spend hours in their company trying to make them see that one another's demands were unreal. In the end, he broke as people do, people who are under constant, extreme stress.

It wasn't as though the stress ended when you knocked off work, as you had to drive home a constant target. At night-time there was constant gunfire, which everyone handles differently. Then you get up the next morning and do it all again. Poor bugger.

One morning, on getting up, our gate guard was extremely upset. His brother had not turned up to take over from him. They were very close and there is no way his brother would not turn up. Up the street from one guard to another, the message came through that the brother had been on his way to work when the army came along and picked a selection of men to fill their water truck with water. He explained he was employed and had to get to work. So, they threw him in the cells and he was in jail.

We discussed who would go and try to buy him out of jail. I was Contract Manager and I had access to company funds. After a few phone calls it was decided that we would go together to buy him out. Straight bribe, no worries. All of a sudden, he came up the street and problem was solved, I never did find out how that happened, arrested one minute and free the next with no money paid.

***

I am amazed at the women who worked for the Red Cross. I was in the office one day to see the doctor—I had some stitches that had to be removed and as I waited for him, they gave me one of their leaflets to read. I was horrified. Most countries run on the backs of their women. Here was no different; the women would be working out in the fields and along would come either rebels, or government soldiers, they would pick a woman and kidnap her. She was to cook for them, wash for them, have sex with any one of them as they chose. If she cried or complained upon moving on, they would insert a gun into her vagina and pull the trigger. This did not always kill her, but most of the time it did. If they were pleased with her, they may release her and her husband, once she had a health check, would take her back, realising she was not to blame.

***

As Contract Manager this tour, I made up the wages for the house staff. I had been advised that one of the gate guards was to have so many frambou (Franc) removed from his wage, I made some enquiries about what this was for. It seems his wife had given birth to a baby that was either still born or died just after birth. The hospital would not release the body of the baby for burial unless they paid forty US dollars. There was a letter from the Red Cross doctor who tried to intercede on his behalf but to no avail. I could think of no greater tragedy—having to pay for the body of your child. They would have just burnt it in hospital waste. I paid the forty dollars as I just could not see them having to pay for that.

***

The South African pilots spent a lot of time with the South African Army who had set up camp at the airport, in order to stop such events as having the multiple rocket launchers aimed our aircraft on approach to land. You are more vulnerable on approach as you are slowing down and descending in order to land, whereas on departure you are accelerating and climbing out of their range. So, the guys would go out there and have a barbeque and beers and more than one of them fell asleep on the grass. They got bitten by mosquitoes and two of our guys got malaria. One of the older guys was not really looking for hours and the FO and I did the week's work; we never worried about the fact that we hadn't seen our colleague over the week. We were on a rotating roster with two captains and one FO. On the day the FO was off, the two captains would fly together. But we all knew that he wasn't real keen to fly, but he wanted to stay in country as the South Africans received a daily allowance on top of their wage for time in country. By Saturday, we asked our chef/houseboy where our missing colleague was. "Oh, he is sick."

I went down to check on him. After knocking on the door with no response I yelled, "I am coming in, if you are or are not decent, I don't care." I entered and could not see him. Then I noticed a grey lump on the bed; he constantly wore grey clothes—shirt, trousers, and he had grey hair and a grey beard. But his skin was grey. I quickly realised this was not good. I yelled at the FO, "He is SICK, REALLY SICK, I am going for the doctor."

While waiting for the doctor, the FO had managed to raise the pilot and get him to the toilet. He said to the doctor, "His pee is black."

Stunned, he said, "Blackwater fever."

This means the kidneys are shutting down and the patient is indeed dying, death follows in the not too distant future. The doctor said, "We have to get him out, NOW."

The Otter is too slow and we knew the company had medevac insurance and we could have a jet sent for him. But that would be at least 10 hours for a flight there and back.

We rang the company and it was decided that we should take money to the airport, and they would arrange a ticket for the flight leaving in one hour and we would get him to the aircraft and boarded. The doctor helped with this. They arranged our handlers at Nairobi to literally pick him up and take him from Nairobi aircraft and put him on the Jo'burg aircraft. It worked—we got him there and all fell into place, he arrived in Jo'burg approximately five hours later and was put on an ambulance at the airport and was being treated in hospital with a specialist soon after. The specialist said, "If we had waited for the Medevac Jet he would have died." The other serious malaria case was put into the local hospital—a military one, because they were the best. When he had his blood test his blood was showing 100% malaria and again the Red Cross doctor came to our rescue. He got him in to the hospital, supplied the sheets, and when we visited, the thing that made us want to run was the blood on the walls. None of us were prepared to stay with him and feed him, so when we went to visit, we took food of some sort, ice cream and stuff from home. But in these hospitals when your drip needs changing you go to the nursing station. They do not come to you.

We did all sorts of flights, but the one that really sticks in my mind is a reunification flight. This is where the children are taken back to the villages they are from after a local war. These children had been removed and we were to take them back. We left Bujumbura and flew to Kigoma just over the border in Tanzania, picked up the children and went to Bukavu. From Bukavu, we flew into Goma Democratic Republic of the Congo (DRC) to get visas for their entry back home in Shawbunda. We then went back to Bukavu to refuel as the trip there and back would take our fuel to the limit. We would land back at Bukavu with reserves on board. We accomplished all of this and on our return to Bukavu having refuelled, I started the engine and out of nowhere came soldiers and they aimed their AK47s directly at the cockpit and gave the sign to close down our engines. We did this and I called the Red Cross coordinator up to the cockpit and pointed to the front of the aircraft. He got out and spoke to them; these soldiers were from the DRC. They informed us if we didn't turn back, we would be shot as the rebels planned to shoot us anyway. The Red Cross knew this to be false as they had agreements with the rebels that we had safe conduct. It was just the DRC stopping any contact with the rebels. Of course, we obeyed as before I came to this area six International Committee of the Red Cross (ICRC) staff had been killed at Bukavu in 2001.

Approaching Christmas, we got pictures of Santa Claus and had Dean, our engineer, stick the pictures of Santa to the aircraft and on arrival at the different strips we would throw out bon bons to the local children. This was a real treat as all family money went to necessities and so approaching Christmas would see more children at the airfields. One of the saddest things I saw was at Gitega—a supposedly international airport used by the president of Burundi in his private jet (the fact the aircraft would not have fitted was of no consequence). Because it was an international airport it had guards and the local children could not enter to get their bonbons so I ran to the gate and threw them to the children. They all hit the ground thinking I was throwing grenades. The airport guard yelled to them, "Bonbons! Sweeties!" And all of a sudden, their fear alleviated, they ran happily to pick up their treats. I have always thought that was the saddest thing. I related this story one day and was immediately set upon by a do-gooder saying I should have supplied fruit. Fruit is a commodity they can get off the trees. Anyway, I give for the heart and the heart likes sweet things. Also, I have yet to meet any of these do-gooders actually in the country taking the risks themselves, just knockers and whingers. As I said before, those that can, do, those that can't, in this case, whinge.

There was another flight in which either the Red Cross or the UN serviced an airport and as they landed the rebels came out of the long grass and slaughtered all, except the pilots. Then made them load the bodies and said, "Get this garbage out of our country." I believe that the Red Cross left that area and still refuses to service that airport. The thing I found interesting was that the Red Cross people all wear small vests with a RED CROSS front and back. We pilots, received no sort of protection like that.

But they would say to us, "You will get us all out if we have to get out in a hurry—won't you?"

***

Another day, the South African Army were on a recovery mission. It seems they had trained some local soldiers in rappelling out of helicopters—they trained a lot of the Burundi military. They were informed that they were now required to do the same over water. There is a very deep river that either runs into or out of Lake Tanganyika. They dropped four recruits from the helicopter with all their equipment. The men sank and drowned. No one had found out if any of these recruits could swim. Obviously, they couldn't, as even with full kit they should have been able to at least make the shore or perhaps someone should have checked the depth.

I still cannot believe how stupid that was and how life is so cheap. They were strong healthy men who died for nothing.

Chapter 29
Algeria

I did a couple of tours in Algeria; I loved the flying—a whole new adventure. On one break the company asked me to ferry an aircraft from Altenrhein Airport in Switzerland to Hassi Messaoud in Algers. I was to do this flight with another captain—a Frenchman—who had been employed by the company as we had gained some oil contracts in Algeria where French was widely spoken along with English.

I was told my French colleague would be given the cash to pay the expenses (such as accommodation, airport fees and fuel). He was currently at Head Office and cash was being given to him almost as we spoke. However, he was a friend of the other French captain who also worked in Algeria. They, between them, decided to raid the money for the ferry to boost the Algerian contract cash. So, a large amount of money was put into that cash fund. The rest he paid on his credit card. He was going to be responsible for the fuel, airport fees, and charges associated with the ferry. I was outraged that money designated for the ferry had been given to the Algerian contract and that he had put the rest on his credit card. I had absolutely no knowledge of the funds available. It was an extremely old Twin Otter and had the funniest instrument layout I had seen. We had been told we were to cross the border into Germany and to buy our fuel there as an international flight the tax of fuel is more favourable and so we departed. First, overnight, was Grenoble—beautiful food, but my accommodation was not good. I had overslept—most unusual for me, but I put it down to being so furious about the money and general attitude.

We left for the airport and on departure we were planning on finding our way down the valleys between the Alps, but even at our low altitudes we were picking up ice. So, we returned to Grenoble and had trouble getting accommodation, as the original place was booked out. So, he hired a car and went to visit his wife in a walled village approximately two hours' drive away. Back to Grenoble so we could make a quick departure the next morning.

This time we got away with no icing problems and were finally away flying in Italian airspace and we refuelled at Sicily. From there it was on to Tunisia. I had done the leg into Sicily so this was his leg. He turned the wrong way on the DME arrival causing lots of upset from tower. We can all do this, orientating in strange airspace with no visual feature and heavy accents. It happens but they got quite annoyed. Then we landed and had trouble finding our parking. After refuelling he announced he had no money on the credit card. "I have spent it all," he said. I had no knowledge of the original amount. But companies know fuel consumption and they allow for problems—overnights and any other expenses and suddenly we had none. The dumb bastard who had given 4000 dollars to his colleague now didn't have money to pay for fuel. The airport began hassling us to depart. I used my personal credit card to pay fuel hoping against hope that it would be refunded by the company. They had a reputation for being very slow to pay. I was not a happy lady.

The GPS was not accepting new destinations as its data bank was full. So, I was frantically deleting waypoints and airports and putting in new coordinates for the rest of the trip. The airport was insisting we depart and so we left with me flying this leg, and also trying to update database, while he did the radio. He was upset at our treatment at Tunisia airport. What he didn't seem to understand was this was a major international airport, and they really didn't want us there. Especially with his level of professionalism, like a lot of French men—he was up himself.

Many years previous, a colleague had turned the wrong way at Heathrow on a Standard Instrument Departure. They had set up the flight director wrong. Heathrow while on the radio remained calm and collected, although they did hear about it later by phone. Here, we were dealing with a far more volatile personality type. They had made their displeasure known for all to hear and he was mortified, he was French and they are far more emotional. Therefore, all errors are hidden.

So, I was fairly busy and feeling frustrated, as it was also new airspace for me. We made our way to Tozeur where we had to go through customs and immigration as we were about to cross the border into Algeria. On the ground, at Tozeur were two B747 which Idi Amin used to escape from Uganda, from there he went to Jeddah. They were just sitting there gathering dust. After passing through customs and immigration we continued on to Hassi Messaoud. Where the aircraft then had to go through customs in Algeria. But by coming in the back door we at least had the aircraft where it would be available to fly as soon as it passed inspection, whereas if we had entered via Algiers the aircraft would have sat there and then a pick up would have to be arranged. Because I had just finished a tour and had been going away on my break when asked if I could help with the ferry, I said, "Yes, love to, but I have these bookings and being here can't cancel; if you can contact them and make everything a week later, I shall do it."

So, for me it was straight onto an aircraft back to London and then on to see friends in Sweden.

Next tour I had in Algeria, we had to go to Hassi El Sheik. On arrival we dropped our passengers off and were told to wait, we had water and were told they would not be long.

We were then informed we could depart and go to the coordinates we were given and told there was a landing area there. We were to land and pick up passengers and take them back to one of the oil camps. As we checked the aircraft, we were very aware of the temperatures, as you cannot start a turbine engine over certain degrees centigrade and it was definitely above that.

We rang the company and said, "We have a problem."

When we explained, the reply was, "You have very hot weather experience, what do you suggest?" But never this hot, but with the company's blessing, I used a technique I had used before in an emergency situation where we had, had to get away. A volcano had been showing signs of erupting and it had already taken out half the runway. We had to go, here similar we had to depart. The technique (the method used was to delay the start until the gas generator wound up to well past the 12/13ng usually used, trying for, if possible, a high of 18/20) I had used before, worked and we started without an overheat. Sure enough at the coordinates were our clients, whom we picked up. We were on our way home to base. I really enjoyed flying in Algeria but I didn't enjoy working with the French crew as they made mistakes and then left you to sort it out. These two were arseholes that took no responsibility for anything. I was just in off the flight from Algers when I was asked if I could fly this afternoon in approximately one hour. You usually arrived, were taken to the camp and had lunch, acclimatised, had dinner, socialised a little, had a good sleep and you were ready to go the next morning. The pilot who was operating today would be on the flight out next day. But no, my French colleague had misjudged his load and put on too much fuel, it was going to cause such an overweight problem that he was not prepared to defuel as that is sheer waste of fuel, and he was not prepared to tell the client he could not carry the required passengers. So, he got sick and left it for me to sort out. Fucking coward, I hated working back to back with these two 'men'.

They also reported my FO for being an alcoholic. In the camps many miles deep into the Sahara Desert, the Westerners were allowed two small cans of beer a night with their meal. Greg use to have just one. I had been told by head office that they had a report from the French captains that Greg, my favourite FO, had alcohol problems and I was to keep an eye on him. Greg and I were flying one day and I said, "Hey, you have been reported by the French, as being an alcoholic." He thought I was joking until his time out, when he was asked to report to the company, who made the accusation to his face.

Next tour we did together, he said, "I didn't believe you, one beer a night. What the hell are they on about?" I never saw him take more than one beer at any time. These French pilots were just shit stirrers and cowards, anything to take the blame off of them.

***

Chapter 30
Haboobs

Even as an Australian it was daunting, our country being one of such large open spaces.

We would often see camels, either in a herd or on their own. One day the head of camp security offered to take me out into the Sahara to visit an old well. We went off in an old jeep. The next thing I knew there were four outriders surrounding our vehicle as we ventured from camp. They were guards from the camp who followed to make sure we were all right. Some of the guards were formerly in the French Foreign Legion and I had been warned that they could be very brutal and to be careful. However, they always treated me very well. We arrived at the old well and I was told it had been there since biblical times. All along the way, curling vines were growing with small marrow vegetables on them and it was these fruits that the camels loved.

As we drove along, I could see an extensive line of grey across the earth like a fault line. The driver pulled up and collected some of the grey soil for me. It is this earth that is used to make mudpacks for women. Many of the large cosmetic companies purchase this earth for their products. They pulled up and gathered some of this earth for me so I could make a face mask. Every time I made myself a face mask, one of the other crews would knock on my door and I would feel such a fool trying to get the stuff off my face and I would answer the door after making them wait. It was like they knew the instant I put one on. I have never tried since. I was also told if the camp came under attack, I was to make my way to head of security and he would be trying to make his way to me.

***

We flew to a place called Reg, this is the flattest place on earth and it was here I experienced my first mirage. It was an amazing experience. Algeria, like most countries, had its own unique weather and I had a new encounter flying in the sandstorms they called the haboobs. We weren't actually flying in them, but if they were forecast, we knew the flight conditions would be turbulent. The sand was also a sure way to ruin an engine. Our soldiers in Iraq mention experiencing these storms. Frightening!

One day, I was paired with Greg, my favourite FO. We were up at ten or eleven thousand feet and we encountered ice. It seemed incredible that we were in the middle of the Sahara Desert and there was ice. On nearing the thunderstorm cell, ice began to form on the aircraft. Greg was ecstatic because he hadn't experienced ice before, but I decided we should get out of there. We descended and went off course to avoid further ice build-up.

Earlier, when I was in Toronto at Bombardier, we were taught about the many Otters that had come to grief in icing conditions in Alaska. The aircraft controls do not act in the normal sense when there is ice on those controls. They proved this in a wind tunnel simulation. So, my desire to keep free from ice was well founded.

***

While there, I was adopted by some of the Algerian women who wanted to learn English. It was funny because I am a female but I also have an excellent command of four-letter expletives and yet they wanted me to teach them English. I certainly had to modify my expressions. While I have long since tempered my language, introduce me to frustration, and it all comes back.

I found these Algerian women completely different to any women I had been with before. When in the company of men, the women are very reticent and yet the women are very bold and immodest amongst other women. If they came to my container (we were living in shipping containers) they made me lock my door because they could not take off their headscarves if it was possible that a man might see them. I found this annoying because my door was always open to my FO and other colleagues, and they were suddenly locked out. The women chattered about my apparent goodness even though my head remained uncovered and open to the world. But once that door was locked, they would often disrobe completely, without embarrassment. I have always been shy amongst my fellow women.

One of the ladies was losing some of her hair and she required injections of some sort of hormone. On the very first night of teaching this lady lifted her robes and bared her bottom in front of me while another gave her an injection in her rump.

Once we became more familiar with one another these lessons became a source of great amusement to me. I had no English-speaking books apart from my novels; John Grisham, Tom Clancy, Colin Forbes, Clive Cussler, and many others. They were definitely not the source of Standard English lessons.

I mentioned this to my colleagues and one said, "I have a copy of 'Who Moved My cheese'?"

I borrowed the book. What a laugh trying to explain a mouse to someone who doesn't speak English. We went through Mickey Mouse, rodents, and in the end, I got it with Tom and Jerry, as that was a cartoon they knew. Then I had to remember which one was the mouse.

I acquired a copy of an English newspaper. I thought this might help being written in English as it should be spoken. How wrong I was. I was leafing through the paper and towards the middle I came across a page of the most scantily dressed women showing off the latest bikinis. I turned that page over very quickly. All of a sudden one of the women said, "Oohhh!"

There was a picture of the actor Harrison Ford. They all thought he was beautiful and wanted to read this story. Unfortunately, the story was about Mr Ford's affair with the actress Callista Flockhart. In the story, the affair was called a 'fling'. Try to explain 'fling' in the sexual connotation to people who do not have English as their first language. Anyway, all of a sudden, the penny dropped that he was having sex with a lady who wasn't his wife. They almost tore the paper up. They started hitting it, while I was still trying to hold it. I am sure Mr Ford lost some fans that day. Another thing I found interesting was that they always blamed the woman. One of the girls had found out that her father was having an affair and declared the other woman a prostitute. Her father was not wrong.

These women were a delight, very enjoyable and willing to be my friends and prepared to accept me, despite me being a bare headed, loud, laughing, woman who treated men as equal, if not less.

***

I met local men in the canteen and when I flew them from Hassi Messaoud to the various camps, I was treated with awe. Initially they were shocked to find a woman captain, especially as I had flown them in some extremely bad weather. At first, I had trouble ordering fuel because taking an order from a female was just not acceptable. But by the time I had finished my Algerian stint, if I said jump, they said, how high?

There were other women pilots but they were FOs, I was a captain. One day we were flying in really bad weather. There was a sand storm approaching. Visibility was rapidly decreasing and it was extremely turbulent. I looked back into the aircraft and witnessed all the worried faces of the passengers as the aircraft bumped and rolled around the sky. I started to laugh and the look of relief that spread around the cabin was obvious. When we landed some of the passengers came up to me and said that I must be a very strong woman not to be afraid. But in reality, it is just bumps. To those not used to it, I am sure it is frightening, but the crew are accustomed to it. I can honestly say that this job was one of my best for challenges.

On another trip, we were to deliver our passengers to various mines and as we approached Tiffernine we were told we could not return to base as they had a sandstorm coming through, and we were to stay for a few hours at the camp. So, all the passengers got off and we were taken to the camp to hang about. As we left the aircraft, we put in all the bungs (these protect the engines and intakes from ingesting sand into the engines) closed the aircraft up tight and tied it down. After a few hours we were told we were to stay the night along with the passengers as Hassi Messaoud had a large sand storm there, we were to stay put. The camps are used to this and we were fed and found sleeping quarters. But the passengers' luggage was still on our aircraft so Greg and I, plus the engineer, made our way back to the airport to get their luggage. Visibility was so bad that the aircraft had been left in the refuelling bay as we thought we would only be a few hours. There were obviously no other aircraft flying so we were not inconveniencing anyone. But on getting to the bowser we could not see the aircraft and we had to tie a rope to the refuelling equipment and head in the direction of the aircraft which we could not see. On getting to the aircraft we unloaded their luggage then followed the rope back to the refuelling point and the jeep we had borrowed. The aircraft could not have been any more than seven meters from the refuelling point. We couldn't see the aircraft from the refuelling point and from the aircraft we couldn't see either the refuelling point or jeep. Once we had the luggage safely stored it was back to camp and the safety it afforded us.

I was told it is the law in Algeria if someone arrived at a camp unannounced it is the law that you must supply fuel, water and shelter if asked.

***

It was truly disconcerting to find out how reviled we were, Greg and I were in the mess one night and over our meal we were talking to an American geologist who was on site for very large periods of time. This evening, 9/11 came up and I remarked how I had been in Angola and we had actually been to the market out of town when we heard. There was no animosity towards us and it was just a shocking news item. However, he had a far different experience as the news came through, he was surrounded by cheering locals baying for blood and the women started making that clucking sound deep in their throats. He unfortunately, had lost a daughter recently through a domestic violence scenario and was still grieving. To find these people relishing in the deaths of so many horrified him. He was suddenly bereft of any goodwill to these people. As he related the story to us, we suddenly realised just how quickly we could be next.

The camp guards were not only there to protect us from the Bedouins who were often camped outside the compounds, but to keep us safe from the local workers also. A lot of them were ex-foreign legion. No loyalties, just money worked with these people.

***

On my last tour in Algeria, I had been sent to one of the camps and it was extremely hot out there in the Sahara Desert. On the first occasion, we were sent to Reg, and we were told to fly over the strip because it had not been landed on since the Second World War. We flew over the airstrip to have a look at the surface and it wasn't too bad, so we landed. But the oil company left Greg and I out there in extreme heat for over four hours. They were such demons in demanding special safety harnesses and special shoes for the crews that washed the aircraft. I was amazed that they were prepared to leave two crewmembers without provision for water or shelter in that heat. Their four-wheel drives were all air-conditioned. As luck would have it, we had our own emergency supplies. But we had no protection apart from some Algerian guards (none of whom spoke English), no toilets, not anything. When I walked from my accommodation to the mess, I would greet the various men and women in the camp. One little man kept saying, "J'adore," that is; "I adore you" in French. I was always in a hurry and so kept thinking he was saying 'thirty-four', and wondered why he thought I lived in container thirty-four. Sometimes, I really am away with the fairies. It was my laugh that they liked. Many would come and have their photos taken with me; I am responsible for more broken cameras than I care to imagine.

The temperature regularly got up to fifty-eight degrees Celsius in the shade. Most of us stayed indoors with the air-conditioning on and the camp was really well appointed. There was a pool table and a gym, all in the cool of the air-conditioning, so we virtually lived indoors when not flying. It was so hot that if the generators broke down, the camp would have to close, as it was unliveable outside.

But life in the camps was different and somewhat social. At one camp we were invited to the Saturday night barbeque, when one of European staff turned up in what I would call a male caftan, white to the floor. As he sat with one leg over the other it was very obvious, he wasn't wearing any underwear. At first, I thought he is just oblivious to the fact that he was showing all he had to show. I moved out of the line of sight and resumed chatting. Immediately, this gentleman also moved, he had this smirk on his face as he tried again and again to get a response. One leg at right angles to his lower leg with caftan sort of bunched on top, again full view, this went on with me moving, and seconds later him moving. It had become obvious he was trying to embarrass and intimidate me in some weirdo manner. In the end, one of the other men said, "For God's sake, go and put some trousers on." He departed to return not long after in normal casual gear. I thought nothing of it besides 'what a fuckwit'.

However, the next day he was one of our passengers and we had been told by the company that we were to act as an airline on scheduled flights and were not to wait for anyone. I had asked for this direction in writing as I have worked with my fellow man long enough to know that this sort of direction is okay if everything is going well, however, the minute someone important is late it is the person following orders that is the one who is in the wrong. I might add that this company was so efficient that I had the letter with that direction within ten minutes of asking for it.

There was no way we were going to lose a contract because we were late. These mining camps had some great guys, ex-SAS and Scottish Guards—big men, fully armed, and you had the distinct feeling of being well protected.

Lo and behold, who should be a passenger on my next trip but Mr Genital Display, today all dressed in work clothes and we were to transport him and others to a particular camp. It was a good airfield and we would have a place to stay, usually shipping containers with air conditioners, microwaves, cool drinks. My FO and I were very conscious of the time and hot as it was, we had arranged to be early. Well, one of the security guards was our driver that day and had us out there early as we had requested. He helped around the aircraft as we got it ready, as we always put the bungs in to protect intakes and engines from the sand that was constantly in the atmosphere. All of this had to be removed before flight. Passengers started to arrive and as the FO closed the door and I started the right engine, here was Mr Genital Display running late. The four-wheel drive came far too close to aircraft as he rushed to make the flight. One of the men responsible for security, they were called Operations Liaison Coordinators (OLCs) a very large ex-Scottish Guard, said to me, "Don't you say anything; I will josh him about being late and tell him how you guys have to run to time."

All of a sudden, this passenger got nasty. While he didn't get physical with me, he started to shape up to my FO. He finally calmed down and got on the aircraft and travelled quietly to our destination. On arrival, he was out of the aircraft calling us, "Fucking drivers," and threatening that he would get us all sacked. We were fucking gone; how dare we leave him. On our arrival, my FO opened the door to let the passengers disembark when 'the big man' took a swing at him and actually landed a blow. Very quickly, other employees stepped in and took him away.

We were suddenly called to report to the camp supervisor whereupon I immediately pulled out the letter, only to be greeted with, "Oh, but you must use common sense; his brother is very high up in the company."

I said, "I have been here two days and I don't know anybody. I arrived on Friday afternoon and flew on Saturday and today is Sunday and he is my passenger. I haven't a clue who anyone is."

But he said, "How could I leave such an important part of their team?" I should have been more selective.

Out came my letter, "Oh yes, I know BUT, his brother is a major player. You cannot leave him."

"But I can leave the Queen? Really? As during my briefing on arrival, I was told we waited for no one, not even the Queen if by some miracle she should be there."

"Okay, let's talk—he punched my FO, he could be had for assault, but let's instead, talk sexual harassment."

Well, that sort of put the cat amongst the pigeons. I said, "I really tried to obey all the orders and rules you laid at my doorstep on arrival. We bent over backwards, then he assaulted my FO and you want us to kiss arse, not happening. I have your letter. Would you like to read it?" Lots of back peddling.

"NO, NO THAT WON'T BE NECESSARY."

"If I am not very much mistaken, you intend to take no action regarding the assault, no doubt this interview is to cover his arse. We left him or almost left him as per your directions and you will say his aggressive behaviour to my FO is a result of the threat of being left."

By now, my anger was growing and I said, "That's it for me. This is the second time that man has shown complete and utter disrespect for me and my crew. I wish to make a formal complaint about his display on Saturday night." I went on, "Even though it wasn't me that he had pushed and taken a swing at, it was my FO. He swore to me, at me, and about me, but you know he is a passenger and I didn't feel it was right that we should complain about that."

But the sexual harassment at the barbeque was different and I had witnesses. So, at the age of sixty I filed my first sexual harassment complaint. Boy, did that cause an upset! My company backed me all the way, although my company's base manager did try to smooth things over, saying to me that our company wouldn't like to lose the contract. "Bah Humbug," as Scrooge would say. In for a penny, in for a pound.

The oil company said that if I proceeded with the complaint that they would take it all the way because they took this sort of matter very seriously. However, the Algerian company who my company used for their Air Operators Certificate (AOC) was horrified that a woman could write such a letter, one which described a man's private parts, as they put it. Therefore, I couldn't be a lady. Boy, did I stir up a hornet's nest. Let me say now that once my complaint got up high enough in the chain of command, the oil company acted quickly and flew a man from the UK to adjudicate. At all times, he acted with propriety and decisiveness.

The perpetrator was dismissed on the spot and all those who had tried to cover up the incident were moved sideways. His brother was told to stop allowing his aides to bully and threaten me and to stop insinuating the matter was my fault. It was also revealed that this man had behaved inappropriately to other women, including some FOs. When I finally acted some of them came to me and said that they had had similar problems with him. When the matter was out in the open and his brother could no longer protect him, some female visitors to the camp also made complaints.

I had done the oil company a favour. I don't think I have ever done anything so difficult. I eventually called back to Hassi Messaoud after his brother's second-in-command had interviewed me. I was always interviewed with at least two men in the room and on one occasion there were three men. I stood my ground. I have complete sympathy for women who have to tell their stories in court. A room with three men was intimidating. But a courtroom?

One of the men actually apologised and said he realised his behaviour was aggressive toward me. I concurred. The boys played out their entire repertoire of interview tricks. They would make a statement and then denigrate whoever spoke next. My main thought was, 'How could they?' Didn't they realise I hadn't come down in the last shower? They kept telling me how devastated the perpetrator was that I could make such a complaint. It is times like that I dislike men; when they stick together in an obvious attempt to denigrate and malign women. They even tried to blackmail me by sending one of the Algerian company representatives to me to threaten that I would never work again.

Ultimately I decided I would write a final letter to the oil company in which I stated that I shall no longer deal with them and that I shall have my story proofread by a solicitor to ensure I was not committing either libel or slander and that I would then send that letter to 'The Times'.

I sent that letter to the company by courier on a Thursday morning. On Thursday afternoon the mediator, previously mentioned, arrived from the UK.

He listened to my story and sacked the perpetrator and the matter was over. I have been told that he probably ended up still employed by his company in just another country or oil camp. From Hassi Messaoud, I left Algeria and didn't return, as I was an embarrassment due to the fact that I knew the names of a man's genitals. I had loved it and have two beautiful sand paintings at home that are three-dimensional. I became disappointed in my FO as he had backed down under pressure. It was not Greg, he had stamina and I know he would go well as a captain. As it was, I did put him up for upgrade to captain. The other FO I would not have put him up for upgrade, as to be a captain you have to be prepared to stand your ground, lives depend on it.

On entering Algeria, you must declare all personal belongings as they can remove them from you if you did not declare them on entering. They want to know where you acquired the valuables and on leaving no explanation means confiscation. I arrived for a flight one morning to be told I was leaving the country so they could reregister an aircraft with an Algerian registration, hence when I finally left the country, I would not have my original declaration as when I left for re-registration of the aircraft they confiscated that declaration. I was very worried about the few belongings I had with me. But there were no problems and I left with all my belongings intact.

But my company sent me back to Burundi which, even with the war going on, was a far more pleasant place.

My Algerian women friends thought it was great that a woman would stand up for herself like that. I often think of them and miss them and their large hearts.

Men who had tried to make me back down were, eighteen months later, offering me a job in the Sudan because they needed someone strong, someone who would stand up and be counted. It turned out; I couldn't accept this position as I was over 60. Another country like Angola where you cannot fly commercially over 60 years of age.

Chapter 31
Bolivia

Quite often in Burundi we would fly as low as possible to avoid giving the rebels time to draw a bead on us. It was not unknown for us to come in with bits of foliage in our under-carriage. One day even a bird's nest—crazy stuff—but we stayed safe, I had often asked when told by some of these young pilots of their exploits, "How many eggs were in the nests?"

However, one day the contract captain and also training captain on the other contract, rang me and said "I had a bit of a mishap today and hit the top branches of a tree going into Kirundi." It was a difficult strip, as there were very tall trees on final approach and I thought he must have clipped the top of the foliage.

But on seeing the wing, he had hit a full-fledged tree branch and the wing had a large 'u' shaped dent in the wing. I just shook my head and thought lucky we still have a wing. Bloody mad. But they were young and invincible, so they thought.

Some of these South African pilots would barrel roll the Otters when empty. These aircraft are not for aerobatic manoeuvres. But no matter how one reasoned with them they would just say done correctly it only pulls 1G. That is not the reaction that you want. The aircraft are old and they may not fail on you but could fail on some other poor bastard who is just flying within its parameters, following the rules. One of the guys was ex-South African air force and the first time we were to fly together, with him as an FO, he said, "Well, we will judge one another tomorrow."

I made the comment, "I don't judge—we all make mistakes—the idea is not to fret over them as it is not the mistake you just made that you should worry about, as you have survived that and hopefully learnt from it. It is the next mistake you make you should worry about, as that one might kill you."

Anyway, when we finished our day's flying together, he puffed out his chest and said "What do you think?"

I remarked, "You are not half as good as you think you are, fucking grow up."

He was one who used to barrel roll the aircraft. What a wank!

After this event, I decided I needed a break. I took off to Bolivia. In La Paz it takes about four days to acclimatise to the higher altitude. I didn't think I would have a problem because of all the time I spent in the air, but I did have a problem and I huffed and I puffed my way around the streets. I went and saw Lake

Titicaca, the Island of the Sun, and the Bolivian Inca ruins and then decided to go to Cusco in Peru and on to Machu Picchu.

I made my way to the beautiful little town of Cusco, from there you catch the train up to where the Inca Trail begins or if you are short of time, as I was, you take the train all the way. I was so disappointed. There was absolutely no atmosphere there at all. I would have liked to go back at night when there were not so many people there. It was beautifully maintained but I thought it would be more natural with more vegetation. I spent the day walking around this home of the old Inca civilisation and finally caught the train back to Cusco and then to Bolivia where I had made arrangements to go to Amazonia.

This was a fun time. I went into the pampas and then into the jungle and I think the pampas was more fun. We went hunting caiman (a member of the crocodile family) by torchlight and sure enough we caught one. It was just a little one but interesting all the same. We let him go, of course. Next, we went hunting for anacondas. Our guide found one and he was bitten. While they are not poisonous, they give a nasty bite that can get septic.

Then we went into the jungle where I was bitten by something nasty and my hand swelled up and was painful for a day or two.

Next it was off to Rio where I saw the famous Christ statue. I was told that these Christs do not have a cross behind them because when the Spaniards invaded these lands, they tried to convert the Inca civilisation by waving their crucifixes as a sign of belief. The Incas decided that when they captured the Spaniards, they would crucify them. This was such a slow and painful death that the Spaniards did away with the crucifixes and so the Christ stands with his arms open in a loving gesture, and hence, they use the term Christ, the Redeemer.

I went and hung out by the beaches in Copacabana and Ipanema. The sea is always good for me as this is where I replenish my energy by laying on a beach and sun baking.

It's the reason I have skin cancers.

Chapter 32
Burundi and a Break in Zanzibar

Back to South Africa before returning to Burundi, I met up with a friend who needed to go to the Australian embassy to sort out his passport. As I had a car he asked if I would mind taking him. While I was waiting for him, I was reading in the reading room when I came upon a foreign office publication that outlined places Australians should not go. Somehow, and I stress it was not intentional, I had been to every country on that list.

I recalled that not long after I was back in Burundi for duty on the Red Cross contract and while I sat having my lunch break, I noted that the peace of the day was constantly broken by the noise of gun and mortar fire. It was worse on some tours of duty. Sometimes a tour was uneventful. Other times scary; on more than one night they actually aimed at the house. We would find bullet holes in the walls and shrapnel in the front garden.

On my return visit, I lived in the Red Cross house and apart from a little gunfire in the street and the noise associated with bombing, it was pretty quiet. Sooner or later you find that life in these conditions continues as normal; we socialised, we managed to go to sleep soundly, and were occasionally awoken by mortar fire. Once, having ascertained that we were not under immediate fire, we would go back to sleep.

One New Year's Eve we went to the best restaurant in Bujumbura and as the fireworks were going off it was hard to distinguish the fireworks from the tracer fire of guns, because they would fire their guns in jubilation. Our engineer Dean left the party early this particular night and got lost on the way home. He ended up in the local jail. The cops had put him there for his own safety.

***

On a break from Burundi, I visited Zanzibar to go diving. I have always liked wreck diving. The wreck there, was in an extremely dangerous area where with a change of tides, things could go badly wrong. I chickened out and did a couple of reef dives and must admit it was still great. Here, the turtles came up and swam along beside you. The sea slugs were the most colourful I have seen. I had dived in Vanuatu and had seen lionfish and many other wonders, and had been cave diving and seen sea snakes. I had also dived the President Coolidge, which sunk up at Santo after running into one of its own mines. I have a t-shirt that says, "I went down on the president." That, of course, was after the Monica Lewinsky episode but here it was so different. I had never seen fish of such colours. I Visited Stone Town, did a couple of tours including one about spices and one on the old slave quarters, which I found upsetting. I also spent time in Kenya where I visited different safari parks. I wanted to also do the Giraffe Hotel and the Masai Mara, but when I went to book the Giraffe Hotel it was closed for a break and it was always the wrong time to see the great migration at the Masai Mara. I still hope to do both of these things.

By now, I had been with the company around three years and I was in Sweden when they sent emails to their foreign staff to say, "Thanks, but we don't need you anymore." I went back to South Africa to pick up my things, sell my car and generally get ready to move on. While I was there, I was approached by a rival of the company I had been with. They offered me a job but, in the end, I didn't take it, as they were paying half of what I had been getting. I have always said if I am going to be shot at and we were, then I wanted the sort of money that makes it worth being shot at. I went to the UK to sort out some stuff there and look for a job.

Chapter 33
Ferry and Grace

I was needed for a ferry flight by the rival of my previous South African company. So, I returned to South Africa, albeit remembering the previous ferry, where I had no idea as to the money available and the problems that arose. They informed me that they would be giving me 35,000 USD in cash to carry with a letter to say why I was carrying such a large amount. Before I went to South Africa, I decided I would do some special shopping in the UK. I thought it would be great if I had a flight bag with a false bottom. I received such funny looks as I went to some of the more exclusive men's luggage stores in the UK. In the end, I bought some black material similar to the lining of a flight case and carefully cut a very firm piece of cardboard, which then covered with the material sticking it so that it was completely covered. On putting it into my flight bag, it was virtually undetectable. I also purchased some carbon paper, I believe it is impossible to get these days, as now they have carbonised paper. But then it was available and while I had been in Vanuatu, there had been an illegal moneychanger who had told me if I ever wanted to send money in an envelope to put carbon paper around it, as the x-ray machine could not see through the carbon paper. Also, these days they have dogs that sniff for money, so smuggling money would be much more difficult. I took these actions as trying to get money through some of these countries means paying constant bribes. The ferry flight involved picking up a Twin Otter in Malta and flying it to Singapore. From there they would pay my fare to Australia. I had a co-captain—such a fun lady. I shall give her the name of Grace, as her name is unusual and she would be easily identified and I have no wish to harm her career.

We had plates (these are the instrument approach sheets of paper called plates) that covered regions from southern Europe to Singapore. These took up a large portion of the flight bag and with the false bottom and the money underneath I went through all the x-ray machines from South Africa to Singapore taking in Frankfurt, Malta, Benghazi, Alexandria, Luxor, Jeddah, Riyadh, Dubai, Ooms, Karachi, Jaipur, Patna, Bangladesh, Myanmar, and Phuket. These days all these plates and charts are kept on your iPad. Newer aircraft have fancy electronic navigation systems, but for the old steam driven like the Otter, most pilots carry their iPads with all the necessary documents on this very portable device.

***

I did not go back to Burundi or work for the new company, but the ferry flight from Malta to Singapore was definitely something to look forward to. You are very alone in countries who have no respect for women, but they honour the gold bars on your shoulders. I assure you we never ventured anywhere without them once we were on our way. Grace was a terrific pilot and a real character. She loved a tipple and as we went outbound on a commercial flight to Frankfurt, she bought up big on duty free spirits. My excuse for having a false bottom was that security that is non-existent to citizens in South Africa. As Grace spotted me and my flight bag, she walked over and introduced herself and said, "Do you smoke?"

"No."

She smiled and said "Thank goodness, we are going to be spending time together and I don't need cigarette smoke all over me. We are not sitting together so I guess we will catch up in Frankfurt, as our flight had been planned Frankfurt–Malta." We chatted away and I told her about the money in the bottom of my bag. Pleased to say, she stood stolidly behind me as we went through security. Flight bag through x-ray, no questions as I looked at the screen, I must admit my bag looked like every other bag. Big sigh of relief. There was no problem with the bag at Frankfurt security either. When we went to take delivery of the Twin Otter, we found that the battery was flat. We started using ground power, but it became obvious that it was not charging and the temperature was slowly starting to rise. NiCad batteries can and do overheat, if they do you have approximately half an hour to get down—great if you are not over the sea. So, I said I was not prepared to take delivery until we had a new NiCad battery. I had seen one explode at Benguela—they had just managed to remove it from the aircraft and the explosion is large enough to take the tail off an Otter. They won't fly without a tail. Three days wait, we were told.

"Right," I said, "we will wait, not going with a faulty NiCad. I will ring the company." All of a sudden, a battery was available and we decided we would depart first thing next morning. Next morning saw us up at sparrow's fart to get going. We were flying to Benghazi, Alexandria. We were hoping for Cairo but it was crazy, the radio was extremely busy, and there were problems on the ground with some sort of attack, so we headed off to Luxor. We visited the Valley of Kings and we saw a couple of tombs, one of which was King Tut. In the late afternoon we headed off to Jeddah and did an overnight there. Both of us were carrying headscarves as we did not want to offend the local people, but we were told to wear our uniforms and gold braid while in this area. It made us honorary men as I understood it. Whatever, it worked and we travelled safely to Dubai, apart from a minor incident while refuelling in Riyadh. While at the time it was rather fraught, now I laugh about it and it was all due to Grace. We had been given prepaid fuel vouchers by the company for travel through these countries, but they would not accept them, as they wanted the American dollars we had. So out of all these countries whose companies had promised they would accept their own vouchers, only one did. All the rest refused steadfastly to accept their own company's vouchers, no doubt selling on the black-market the Yankee dollar. Well these men hadn't come up with anyone as determined as Grace, she was one very determined young lady. She refused to hand over the dollars I had given her to pay for fuel and was calling them ragheads straight to their faces. God bless her little cotton socks. Corrupt bastards, ragheads etc., I could hear all of this as I sat in the administration office sorting out flight plans. The phone rang and I could hear an extremely loud altercation between Grace and these refuellers.

"They have no money," the refueller was saying, Grace chiming in with, "We have your company's vouchers, you corrupt ragheads." Things were starting to look exceedingly hostile with talk of prison and things confiscated etc.

I immediately chimed in with, "No, I have the money, I shall pay you here and now and pulled a wad of US dollars from my top pocket. It was our habit to take 5000 USD each morning from the hidden section in my flight bag, returning what was left at the end of the day's flight. All smiles, calm again, we completed the transaction and we were on our way. Next stop Dubai. It was Grace's flight leg and I was doing radio, when one of the controllers in the Dubai approach said "Is that you, Jacinta?" He heard my Australian accent and thought I was a lady called Jacinta Hennesy—an Australian pilot whom he obviously knew."

I said, "No."

"Well, you are an Aussie female, so who are you?" I hadn't worked this part of the world so I was new to him. There was a quick chat and then it was back to business. We landed at Dubai and our handlers here were wonderful. They fed us with coffee and tea and arranged transport as well as an engineer for a problem we had with the propeller.

***

"Lots of oil in the front locker, what is this for?"

"Oh, the left-hand propeller hunts a bit."

This meant it cycled as it tried to put itself into feather. The engineer supplied by the handlers was excellent and fixed this problem in no time. He could have taken longer as we became stuck in Dubai, where we had to stay for 12 days while the company sorted our visas to travel through India. The engineer had a look at the left propeller and it was an O-ring—not seated correctly and leaking oil, which was causing the problem. Not very funny when you are over miles and miles of water—the Gulf of Oman, just above the Arabian Sea as we flew Muscat to Karachi direct.

Just before we departed from Dubai, while I was paying airport charges, the phone rang and the man working out the charges said, "Your colleague just had your aircraft window washed and for this he increased the account by 100USD." On getting back to the aircraft Grace said, "I just had our window cleaned."

I said, "Yes I know."

"How?"

"They increased the bill by 100 USD." I just about had to pick her up off the ground.

The problem with the visa for India was that some time before a rebel group had used a Twin Otter to drop bombs on a part of India and they didn't want to allow another Otter through. When we finally got our clearance, it was extremely late in the afternoon, having already been up all day to suddenly get planned and away was going to be difficult. We went to our handlers at Dubai airport and planned to Karachi, leaving early next morning having to first land at Omms (Muscat) where they did accept our prepaid fuel vouchers. But in order to make our time slot for entering Indian airspace we had to depart Karachi at 0300 Karachi time. We worked 21 hours that day and finally landed at Chittagong in Bangladesh. We had landed at Karachi, where Grace had an upset tummy and as we were coming into land, she desperately needed a toilet, so as we neared the parking area, I pulled up to let her out and she ran to the handler's car asking to be taken to the toilet. However, they would not leave me to park and tie down and refuel the aircraft for our early morning departure. Grace was in such a rush to make the terminal after the aircraft was closed down and I had grabbed my overnight bag. We were leisurely driven to immigration. Grace was frantic.

It was early evening as we entered the hotel. Security was tight as there had been a bomb attack that had killed staff and guests three days before. We ate, slept and showered and we were up at 0130 hours to get to the airport and depart. We landed at Jaipur where we were greeted with, "We expected you yesterday." We asked if there was somewhere, we could buy lunch and coffee.

"No," they said, but the controllers made us a coffee and gave us half their sandwiches, which we ate with gusto as we had had nothing to eat for the last 10 hours. They took our money for charges and refuelling and we departed after being treated with much kindness; there wasn't anything they wouldn't do to help us. Professional in their attitude, they were great people to deal with, giving information on what to expect with the rest of the flight across India. Our next stop was Patna and again we were treated very well. This was our last stop before moving into Bangladesh airspace. Next stop, Chittagong, we landed late and had to go through immigration. We closed the aircraft up and followed through to immigration where we were told we had to leave in 72 hours. Crew badges give you three days in a country without any problems, but we needed five days and this involved having to write a begging letter, asking to be allowed to stay. As we handed across our passports there was a small stipend included. The reasons we needed five days was, we were not allowed to enter Burmese airspace till a particular date. The delay crossing India had a flow on effect to the other countries. As he looked at my passport, he declared it wrong, there was a mistake. I said, "No, what is wrong?" At this stage I was 62.

He said, "They have your age wrong."

I said, "No, not possible, here is my ID—it shows the same birthdate."

"No, it is wrong, people here who were born in 1941 are either very fat or for the long sleep."

I laughed and said "Well, sorry but it is correct." We were allowed to stay and five days later, I had to write a begging letter to be allowed to leave, having overstayed with permission our crew badges' time limit. It was here in

Bangladesh that I paid eight hundred US dollars to have a conveyor belt brought to the aircraft, so we could walk up it to check the oil. They had no ladders and would not allow us to use the refueller's ladders. I had gone out early the next morning to check the aircraft, as we had been rushed the night before. We were the last flight in and they had wanted to close up and go home. So, next morning, I went out alone as Grace had told me she intended to sleep in, since we had worked 21 hours straight.

Next stop was Myanmar, as we taxied off the runway, I misunderstood a direction from airport ground which controls surface movement (SM) and they got so nasty. They were, and I think still are, military, but rude and made sure we knew we were not welcome. We refuelled and left as soon as possible.

One morning, I opened my flight bag and I noticed a tiny piece of carbon paper was showing from the false bottom. I had been so lucky that during the previous night's search it was not discovered. Next stop was Phuket—down the Bay of Bengal into Thailand and then to Phuket. Such beautiful scenery, so many little islands and we were now so close. We were almost to Singapore, but not before we had an evening in Phuket. We went out to a food market and pigged out. Early next morning, we were heading to a little airport North of Changi, the main Singapore airport. I overnighted there before catching my flight on to Brisbane and home. We rang the company to say the aircraft had been delivered and they were so happy to have it there safely that they doubled my salary. I gave the change to Grace to take back and I hope they did the same for her.

***

When I travel to South Africa, I always look her up and we meet and have a great laugh. Hiding the money might sound exciting but it was Grace that caused the laughs. She had many litres of alcohol in her bags and we were going through all these Muslim countries and because we left the bottles airside and did not go through their borders with it, they couldn't do anything. We were on international soil and until we take it into their country, they can do nothing, at no stage did we attempt to take her alcohol landside. Grace would just laugh and say, "It is in my bag and you cannot touch me."

She also had a whirlwind romance in Dubai and called most of the gentlemen she met, 'ragheads'. She was terribly racist and I spent much of my time trying to gloss over some of her more outlandish exploits. However, she didn't have a mean bone in her body and on many occasions actually helped out these men she treated so disdainfully, so I tended to overlook the racism and put it down to bravado.

We said our goodbyes. She was going home to South Africa but I think she was having a few days in Singapore first. It was a great trip.

Chapter 34
Home—Australia

After my return from the ferry flight, I started looking for another job and, in the meantime, I talked to my old boss at Bunbury Flying School and was invited back there. Blair has been wonderful to me. Great family man, who had overcome hardship by putting his nose to the grindstone and working his butt off. Like most Australians, he just buckles down and works harder when the going gets tough. How come this man owns a flying school? Well, he was a member of the local aero club and he was and still is innovative and suggested how they could improve. Some people don't like change and don't want to improve, familiarity breeds contempt. So, they banned him and he decided then and there that he would start his own school. Right from the start, the instructor he hired was full of shit, lied and cheated and lasted just long enough to thoroughly piss Blair off. It was during this time I met Blair and I found him to be an upfront, honest guy. He liked my no-nonsense approach and I helped him out more than once and so he reciprocated and gave me work when I returned from overseas. So here I was back again—yes, I went to work for him. When I arrived, I didn't have a lot of students, so I decided that I would run a few courses and I gained a few students. I was flying and enjoying it again. I love imparting knowledge. I was enjoying a quiet life when I saw a job in China being advertised. Blair and his family were wonderful to me and I know his school is still operating. I hope it continues to do so as if anyone deserves the best, this man and his family do.

Chapter 35
China

I had to go to New Zealand for the interview. I was successful and I was truly looking forward to going to China to take up the position of CFI. We initially worked in Beijing but were told we would be moved to Hebei province, Shijiazhung Zhengding Airport. I met the gentleman who had been hired by a Chinese consortium. He had been operating the Pan Am flight training school in the US. Pan Am, the airline, had long since gone out of business, but the school had somehow survived, as by this time it had become a separate entity. One of the things I was most looking forward to was working with people who have the same work ethic as I do. Boy, how wrong was I? I was suddenly working with people who were the laziest I have ever met. Two-hour siestas. It took three people to do that job, in Australia, UK or US, one semi-proficient person could have done on their own. However, in their defence, I later found out that their pay was so poor that to work hard would undermine the system. If you employ one efficient person to do the work that they employed three people for, then the general economy would take a beating.

On arrival things were not as promised. What the Chinese call a three-star hotel would not have received a one-star rating in any other country. I was also given an assistant who was an American Chinese, who obviously still had some relatives in China, as he thought himself above all of us and we were supposed to call him Mr when he called us by our first names. He was a liar and when we finally did get aircraft, he took one while drunk one night and went flying. The Caucasian instructors would have been thrown in jail for such an infringement. With Mr D (not real name but his name sounded like an initial) it was hidden and kept quiet. Knowing one of the other instructors was allergic to peanuts, he ordered meals that had peanuts in some form in all the dishes we ordered on a night out. One of the other young men who spoke Chinese heard him alter the orders for food. Knowing that the allergy could have killed the other instructor— it was a despicable act by a very irresponsible young man. Every time a student went solo, and believe me it was hard getting them solo, as they would only allow one aircraft up at a time—and if we moved more than 500 metres off track, we were accused of spying. But every time a student went solo, I had to go to the tower; if one killed himself, the foreigners were going to be blamed. Only once did I have to take over the microphone and talk to one of the students. At the last minute, the student would panic and go around, so after about the fifth time I took over the microphone and talked to the student, calming him. Yes, he bounced on landing, but so what? The aircraft flew again and as we say, any landing you walk away from must be a good one; if you can use the aircraft again that is a bonus. The student came running down the tarmac yelling "Sorry, sorry!" But when I brushed it off saying it happens, he had the biggest smile I have ever seen, and since he was the last student of that class to go solo, we had a barbeque and a slip and slide which was put together by the New Zealand instructors.

Then came along the Chinese security, and tried to make us stop having fun as they said the grass hadn't been paid for. We had sought permission for this event and to be told we could not 'as the grass hadn't been paid for' was unbelievable. On checking with the 'boss', he enquired directly to the owners and it seemed the grass had been rented. That story is true, as are all the rest but if one was to be disbelieved this is the one, I reckon it would be. Some of the students followed me home that night, saying that they had a wonderful time and they would remember it all their lives. There was laughter in the young men but it had been suppressed and for that I think the Chinese should be ashamed of themselves. Laughter is such an important part of our development. If you can laugh even in the direst of times there is hope for you.

The student was a delightful young man and quite the favourite as he tried so hard. He should never have passed the English language assessment from the International Language school as he passed with 3%—by that I don't mean pass mark was 50 and he got 53. His mark on the exam was 3, but if he had been marked a fail someone would have had to answer. So, pass him off to the foreign instructors, let them fail. But we worked with him and we worked on a rewards system, hence the parties and barbeque that I paid for. The Chinese work on a punishment system. I can truly say I was hated by many of the Chinese in authority by the time I left.

One young man called Hawk used to say I was just a nasty old woman, well he may like to know I kept his business card, as on it instead of putting consultant, he introduced himself as a 'cumsultant'. That gave me a laugh. I still have that card and still chuckle.

The American boss was as useless as tits on a bull. Any time I said we are being discriminated against and we were, he would say, "Don't say that." What I wanted to know was why not? Is it only okay to cry discrimination when you are Asian/ black/ brown/ whatever but never white? Or as in Australia, a young heterosexual woman was not allowed to join a lesbian ladies cricket team and when she took it to Human Rights, she was told she had no case, since as a heterosexual she was in the majority. What a load of absolute shit. It is discrimination or not? We are racist. Give me a break. We were so keen to help and work with these young people, and the Chinese blocked us at every turn. We were treated as racial inferiors and we were discriminated against. I had four instructors jailed because they were white. Most of the instructors were New Zealanders. They were really good instructors, who soldiered on, in appalling living conditions and impossible working conditions. We were constantly lied to, belittled and treated with disdain.

One was crossing the road on a green light when a car came through on a red-light, albeit slowly. He hit the instructor who bounced off the bonnet and broke the windscreen. Our instructor was jailed until we paid for the windscreen.

Another was told to get out of the aircraft at the holding point as he informed the tower that the student was to go solo. As he walked across the movement area having been told by the tower to do so, he was arrested by airport security.

Two others were arrested as one of my instructors had a similar build to one of the Russian pilots and they accused him of stealing from the gentlemen's shop. I had a frantic phone call saying, "We need our passports, as they prove we weren't even in the country on the day of the theft." The guy who was accused was a new instructor and had only arrived in the country days before, long after the alleged theft. Why was he accused? He was white.

So, come on, tell me about racial prejudice and discrimination and that's before I start on the female stuff. This American who was supposed to support our efforts did nothing. I do believe at one stage he had been in the diplomatic corps. He did not like my swearing or straight-up approach. We had been hired as foreign experts, but were then told we could not be experts because we had not been trained in China.

We taught emergency response, i.e. what to do when an engine fails in flight or on take-off. I have had both happen and never had an injury to passengers or students. The advantage of training for these emergencies is that when it happens the training takes over and you will survive it. Long before we were hired as instructors for this new flight training school, a very senior instructor (twenty years' experience, a so-called expert) died because he had no training in emergencies. At the government flying school this expert had killed not only himself but also his student in an engine failure after take-off. He tried to hold the aircraft in the air. Of course, they died. No power, nose high, resultant stall, you fall out of the sky, which is exactly what they did. So, they died. Sad, but it happens.

Here again there were Russians, they flew in most weeks, bringing arms and missiles, which I found interesting as China being a world power, I thought they would have made their own armaments. My instructor who had been arrested wrongly as he had not been in the country, looked very much like one of the Russian pilots—both were big bears of men with shaggy bearded grey hair. This particular Russian gentleman loved vodka and would often be seen nursing his bottle lovingly.

One night, as we made our way home here was the Russian on his knees crying and trying to lick the ice onto which his bottle of vodka had fallen—the contents spilling onto the ice. We dragged him off as there had been glass slivers and his tongue would have been badly sliced. One of the other instructors gave him a small bottle of whatever he had and we got him safely into the hotel. The number of times I have heard western pilots say they have to be drunk to fly that Russian shit is numerous. Personally, I believe the Russians make very strong aircraft, maybe not pretty but definitely tough.

I was presented with a Chinese gentleman whom I was supposed to hire to teach the students English; what a fucking joke! When he arrived for interview, my translator suggested he sit in on the interview. I was a bit stunned by this. Thinking if he is to teach English then he should be able to converse with me. Guess again, the man spoke no English at all and I asked my translator to ask how he intended to teach English when he spoke no English himself. He said he would teach English in Chinese. I came very close to getting mad that day but no I just had a swear to myself, saying it was a WAFTM (Waste of Fucking Time and Money) total and complete waste of time not only for me but for the elderly gentleman. I was swearing more than ever in sheer frustration. We had two instructors arrive from the US. Nice people, both very experienced, twin aircraft instructors. They stayed one day, as when they arrived down at Shijiazhuang Airport, they were introduced to me when one of the usual catastrophes was taking place and they offered to get out of my hair. They wanted me to point them to the two Kingairs (type of aircraft) that the boss had told them were waiting for them to fly. The latest Beechcraft Kingair.

"What Kingair?"

"He told us there were two Kingairs here waiting to be flown."

"Really, well, would be nice if he told me. There are no Kingairs here."

"He promised us all the Kingair flying."

"Congratulations! If you can find them you can fly them." The American boss could not believe when he arrived back from Beijing that the two pilots had left.

"What do you mean they have gone?"

"Well, they looked for the two Kingairs—one for her and one for him; they couldn't find them and asked me where they were. I answered honestly and said they weren't here. I arranged for them to see around the airport so they could see for themselves that there were no Kingairs. They were not interested in normal *ab initio* instructing and told me the next morning, they were returning to their old positions."

***

This American man could not believe that they left. The fact that nothing he had told them was true had nothing to do with it, as far as he was concerned. These people came in good faith; he threatened the young instructors that he would ruin their aviation careers if they didn't stay, and still they left. Very much a diplomat—tells them what they want to hear and before they get it, takes it off of them. They had travelled half-way around the world on a bunch of promises to find nothing they had been told was true. Did they also think that the instructors already there wouldn't want to fly the 'Kingairs'?

Yes, we were the very first free enterprise flying school in Red China. We were lied to, treated with complete distain and generally kept in the dark. I don't know who was worse—the American or the Chinese. What I do know is, neither told the truth. We had been promised maximum flight hours in the first 12 months and while we often had to wait idling the engines for 45 minutes before they would let us up (not good for aircraft as the pistons glaze over) they also had the wrong octane fuel and they allowed one aircraft at a time in the training area and when really generous, three in the circuit, but we all had to land when a passenger carrying aircraft arrived. I have never worked in such dreadful conditions—the constant lies, the constant bullshit of the American was beyond comprehension. Then the first solo cross-country students were supplied with contaminated fuel at Tianjin, were we had arranged for away from base refuelling. The fuel was delivered in old drums, completely expired. Fuel in drums has a precise way of being stored—there was no sign that any of these regulations had been adhered to. We raised this concern but there was no action until some solo students had engine problems. It never happened when an instructor was on board, as they didn't really need fuel, it was an exercise to teach them about refuelling and the need for checks. The students did well, the authorities should hang their heads in shame. Fuel in China is expensive—yes, I know it is expensive in every country. But here, the fuel man needing bribing on top of fuel charges for every aircraft he refuelled, making it dearer than Europe. Between the American CEO and the Chinese hierarchy, they couldn't have run a piss-up in a brewery.

We were blocked at every step; they did not want the WESTERNERS to succeed as that would have shown them up. So, they decided that they would not open the gate onto the tarmac until we started the engines and the tower wouldn't give us start clearance until the gates were open.

The instructors had been given the most dreadful rooms in the hotel. I still have photos. One instructor had been in a room where someone who was drunk had thrown up and it had never been cleaned. Another instructor asked me to take the agent to his room, as he wanted to show her his bathroom. The ceiling had fallen down on him while he was taking a shower. When the agent was introduced to me, I said, "I wouldn't be in your shoes for all the tea in China. No pun intended."

"Why?"

"Well, the instructors have been contacting you and complaining, correct?"

"Yes, most annoying—three-star hotel and they are complaining."

So, I took her to meet the instructors who gave her individual tours of their rooms. I have never seen anyone so animated as she was when she next met Mr America. He was backpedalling so fast he had been given a suite of rooms and had arranged the same for her, never realising just how shocked she was at the rooms the instructors had been put in.

One of the instructors took ill while there. The problem was that he had sleep epilepsy which he didn't know about. But this night he had his girlfriend from Australia visiting and was seen to undergo a fit. She had obviously never seen an epileptic fit before and was screaming for help. They called me and I recognised it for an epileptic episode. We called the local hospital that was at the back of the hotel. They refused to treat him, as they said, "he was a drunk Westerner." It was so obvious he was sick and they wouldn't help. Please, please tell me about racism because we were suffering from it. With sleep epilepsy, it only happens when they are tired and feel a bit off and fit and fall asleep where they are, when they wake later, they usually think they have just fallen asleep on the sofa or wherever and think that is the reason they feel unwell.

I arranged for this young man to get to Beijing for a specialist at the International Medical Centre and it was decided to send him home for further medical investigation. He was my responsibility; we also had an ex-NZ nurse who was a flying instructor and this useless arsehole wouldn't help in anyway. No wonder he is no longer nursing. Unfortunately, the instructor lost his licence. By that, I mean unfortunate for him, as he was a born aviator. He had paid to get to the stage he was at in aviation and I had written him a reference and fielded a telephone call from a very good airline and recommended him wholeheartedly. He had just been told he had been accepted when all of this came to light. He lost everything. However, for future passengers it was definitely the correct remedy; as I say you must be medically A1 to fly and hold a licence.

By this time, I'd had enough. I went on a break and got another job. I resigned while I was on break and went back to pack up and leave. The two greatest twits in the place arranged to ship me out at 0400 hours rather than have the students protest. It didn't work as the students got up anyway to say good-bye. I was nothing special, I just treated them like human beings, which is more than their own race superiors did. When I left China, I vowed never to eat Chinese food again, but I do like it and have relented.

I enjoyed China. I enjoyed the food, the man in the street and the students. I did not enjoy the bureaucracy, the charges of spying if we flew slightly off course. How were we to teach lost procedures when if we went off track, we would find ourselves escorted back to base?

Mr America got the sack as they had employed another American as I had been talking of leaving and he also kissed arse. I thought that the original Mr America had no internal fortitude, in other words he had been castrated by the great US Dollar and his desire for it. Such people shouldn't be allowed to work in aviation. Yes, companies need to make a profit but selling your soul to the devil is not on. That is greed.

Chapter 36
War Between the UK and the USA

I went back to the UK to take up a position with an American company who had a base there. I love the UK, no problem with English unless far North amongst the Geordies. So broad, "Yuh Canna understand 'em." What a dreadful position to be in working for a company that knew they invented aviation but working in a country that perfected it?

Yes, the Brits did perfect it. (I have worked in many countries.) I consider the British aviation scene to have the best standards in the world. Their controllers are magic, the aircraft are maintained to the best standard I have seen. Yes, they are a little pedantic, but they get the results. They are honest. So we, the employees of this organisation, were the meat in the sandwich. My manager to start was a really nice man. I think he was Pakistani—a real gentleman and you could talk to him. Sadly, he left and was replaced by a German man who had his favourites, people who started after me got pushed ahead of me because they were men. There was real discrimination in his section and I complained about always being put to the back of the training schedule for actual aircraft. His second-in-command spent more time outdoors having a cigarette break than he did instructing but still the favouritism existed. His best friend put me in the Kingair simulator and then on a single engine approach, he gave me a fire on the go-round. When I did not extinguish the fire he asked, "Why?"

I had silenced the bell. I just laughed and said, "I am on one engine and you simulate a fire, what the hell do you expect me to do? If I shut that one down I am just a very heavy glider." The Kingair doesn't have a magnesium wing, so the chance of it burning off was minimal. The old chieftains and Navajos in the Piper range did have magnesium spars and the wing did burn off, you had just minutes to get down.

He laughed and said, "I shall improve the weather and see if you can get back, I will keep the engine on fire as I want to see how you handle both engines out." You would never do this to a student so as I turned the aircraft with a low angle on bank, he improved the weather (simulators are great that way). I could now see the runway and returned and landed safely. All in a simulator, so really proved nothing except I think and I can fly. He himself admitted he couldn't do it. This arsehole still works at this company—shows what being a 'yes man' can do for you. I complained regarding the discrimination, the fact that a new-to-the-team man was to be given actual aircraft flying for his endorsement while I still hadn't. I also pointed out the fact that yes, Mr Brown tongue got in early but with his constant cigarette breaks actually worked approximately a quarter less than the other staff.

I was sacked. DISCRIMINATION—what a dirty word, especially when dealing with the Americans.

But before I was sacked, I had been sent to Dallas, Texas and then to Wichita in Utah, I enjoyed my time there. My colleagues were great people and I just wish we had the same sort of camaraderie with the UK staff.

I had already booked a ticket to fly to Hawaii to catch up with a friend. I have just had a similar catch-up with the same friend in Portugal, he and his partner spend much of their time in Europe from March to June when the weather is unbearable in Thailand. The thing I have enjoyed most about my job is the people I have met and how we have stayed in contact for so many years. I laugh at my friend as his now partner is his ex-wife and two more compatible people I have yet to meet. They did also visit South of France to catch up with me one year.

***

Chapter 37
Home Again

So, I went back to Blair and settled in to work instructing again. They had another instructor there; he was a New Zealander and not my favourite person. I found out very quickly, he was a bully and his wife did nothing but bitch. One day, I was there holding the fort when she came to visit. I realised later it was by design. Hubby was on a day off and the chief pilot was on days off. He was a lovely man and an extremely proficient instructor and CFI. But at that time, I was on my own, as the weather wasn't pleasant and apart from a few students popping in and out to ask questions and make bookings, I was it.

As she greeted me, I said, "Would you like a coffee?" Receiving an affirmative nod, I went out to put the kettle on.

She wanted to talk, so she began with, "Why does everyone dislike Cyril and I?"

I enquired, "You really want to know?"

"Yes, we really want to know."

"Well, I haven't been here long, but from what I hear, both you and Cyril keep telling us how everything we Australians do is wrong—we have a barbeque every Friday night. I have been to a couple and every time I hear you or Cyril telling us how New Zealand is better—you didn't last on Norfolk Island because of same attitude—you think they are all inbred. Then you come here and the same sort of attitude—if you really feel we Australians are so inferior, can I point out the aircraft flies in both directions—to and from New Zealand. In your short time here today, you have knocked Australia Post, the local shopping centre and the garage where you get fuel. People get sick of being told they are stupid, inferior or whatever else is your gripe today—if you don't like it, go home. As I said the aircraft flies both ways and there are even Air New Zealand flights, so you don't have to travel an Australian airline." I must admit there are times I am a bit too honest, but did she take notice? No way, they both continued on their merry 'We-hate-Australia-and-Australians' campaign.

***

I was asked to pick up a Jabiru (a very light aircraft) from the outback. It had been in an accident and had been sent to Arkoola in South Australia for repair. I was carrying avgas in jerry cans and was to fly across Australia, in this shit heap, which is what I think of Jabirus. It had a wooden propeller and I was told to stay out of the rain as the props sometimes fell apart if they got wet. Having been told by a CASA inspector that you could almost guarantee an engine failure in the first 250 hours depending on which engine they had in them, I was not impressed but thought, *'What the hell? Give it a go.'* But apart from that it had a good DG (directional gyro) and they thought it had a GPS in it, so no worries. On arriving at Port Whyalla I was met by the engineer who took me to the hangar and his home, where I was fed and billeted for the night.

Next morning, saw me up early checking the Jabiru over to depart not much later for Ceduna. I had been told there was rain about but just showers, so I should be able to fly around them. However, if I couldn't do this, to throttle back as it would protect the propeller, only having a few hours in this aircraft. I listened intently to all I was told. On inspection, I noticed the compass was unserviceable and the GPS had departed for parts unknown. The DG worked but they precess and have to be constantly referenced to the compass, which as I said was unserviceable. Joy of joys. I had thrown in a small hand-held GPS that I owned. So, as I lined up the runway, I checked the DG was aligned with runway heading and departed. Forty-five minutes later, I ran into a line of rainstorms with no way through. To avoid the rain, I picked the lightest areas, throttled back and headed through. The rule is if you can see through the rain you can go through it. All of a sudden—clear blue skies—and I continued on to Ceduna. Quite some distance from Ceduna I started to experience a small vibration in the aircraft. When I had been learning helicopters I had been told about vibrations and how dangerous they were and while the aerodynamics of the fixed wing type aircraft and a helicopter are so completely different, it was still a vibration that shouldn't be there. I immediately found a made road heading in the same direction as me, as I checked my GPS, which I only turned on every half hour trying to conserve my battery. I noticed my track to Ceduna and the direction of the road were very similar so I continued to fly the road as a possible landing ground in case I needed a place to carry out a forced landing. Up ahead I could see the sun reflecting off something and thought 'Ceduna'. I arrived overhead, did the join-to-join the circuit and landed, taxiing to the fuel bowser to refuel. On refuelling, I started to hand pull the Jabiru away from the refuelling area so I could have a good look at it. As I put my hands on the propeller at the hub I noticed the ends were starting to shred. This was the cause of the vibration and so I took the aircraft to a tie down area, got a taxi and headed for the township.

***

When I had departed to go and pick the aircraft up, I had been told not to hurry as things were a bit quiet and there was the CFI and Cyril to hold the fort. Now, when I rang in to inform them of the problem, I was told Cyril had come in the day I departed, and said he had a helicopter job for eight weeks and seeing as he was building his hours on helicopters, he was going to have the eight weeks off. So, I had to get back as soon as possible. Well, the word went out and within a few days a local man had rung the boss and said, "I have new propeller for your

159

model Jabiru. I can give you this one and when you buy the new one, deliver it to me." This is Australian mate-ship at its best where you help out the guy in strife. So, the propeller was delivered to me and I went to the local RAC garage in Ceduna and spoke to the mechanic and told him what I needed done. Much scratching of head, "Am I breaking any rules?"

I gave him my phone and the 'how to book' on Jabirus and said, "Here, ring my boss." My boss assured him that it was quite legal for him to do what I was asking and it was arranged that the next day; his first job was to put on a new propeller on this Jabiru. As he did so with me giving the odd encouragement and passing him any tool he asked for (much like a surgical nurse if it went wrong the likelihood was that the person on the table would be me). As he read, he noticed that there was a method of making sure it was aligned correctly. He didn't have the correct tool for that. So, we rang the boss again and with good old Aussie ingenuity these two men worked out how to achieve what was needed with what they had. I then took the aircraft to an area on the airport where I ran that engine's RPM as high as allowed. No vibration, all good and I was on my way again. The Jabiru propeller is made from what looks like a chipboard which they then place a wooden laminate over with a plastic sleeve over that, but at the end of the sleeves, the propeller is open to the weather, hence the failure. I have since found out you can get metal propellers these days. No wonder these aircraft kill people. As it was getting on in the day, I overnighted at the Nullabor roadhouse/motel. It had aviation fuel and a place to sleep and park the aircraft. It was extremely busy, as it catered for the road trains (a road train is an extremely large truck that has at least two trailers attached a usual length is 53.5 metres), motor vehicles and aircraft crossing this barren area of land mass that runs parallel to the Great Australian Bight.

***

Up bright and early and on my way to Kalgoorlie; I had found an airfield where I could refuel close to a mining town. While they didn't have fuel, I had my jerry cans full of avgas all I had to do was transfer it. Finding a strip, I landed and quickly got the fuel out and suddenly realised my hands were not strong enough to undo the caps on the Jerry can. No worries I thought, I shall run to the mine and see if I can get some help. As I ran past the entrance, I noticed a particular lack of personnel. I entered and saw that there were signs of habitation—the mess was laid out for lunch and there were beds not yet made but no people. By this time, I was getting rather frantic as by waiting for lunchtime when the miners would come to be fed, I would lose precious hours. As I ran through the various huts, I spotted a man going into a building that turned out to be an office.

He was very surprised to see this female burst into his office. As I explained the situation, he couldn't have been nicer. Did I need cold-water, fruit, anything? Yes, I need help with my aircraft. He immediately said, "No worries love, I will do what I can." True to his word he put me in his truck and he not only took the tops off the jerry cans, he used the truck bed to stand on as he refuelled the aircraft for me. He stood there and saw me safely off. Next stop Kalgoorlie.

Kalgoorlie is famous for the large gold nuggets that have been found in the area. It still mines around 300 tonnes annually. It was also famous for its street of madams. Hay Street, the red-light area of Kalgoorlie, reminds me of similar streets I have seen in Dusseldorf, where the ladies sit in windows so their clients can window shop.

I did an overnight at the closest motel to the airport and after refuelling I was off once again to make for my home airport. I rang to say I would be arriving that morning with one more refuelling stop to make. I was told no hurry; Cyril was back some two days after departure, surprising everyone with his return. He confided to one of his students he had greened the helicopter up. I said nothing but thought they do not sack you for greening up a helicopter unless you have done something really stupid. Yes, he had his mobile out trying to show how good he was and filming himself flying the machine, when he paid more attention to his filming than flying. What a fuckwit! So, they dispensed with his services and to my knowledge he never flew a helicopter again, as people do not hire idiots.

I made this whole trip by resolutely holding heading on the DG and turning on my GPS. I had purchased new batteries for it at the roadhouse so sometimes left it on for longer periods. Made me thank goodness that my instructor all those years ago had made sure I knew how to navigate.

Back to instructing and living life, walks along the beach and flying. Our little airport was busy and used to host different events such as gliding, with clubs visiting. During one such visit a man came in and said, "Remember me?"

I said, "Of course," but in reality, I didn't have a clue. He prattled on about how I had taught him to fly, I was still scratching my head when he reminded me of his name and said, "Let's go gliding."

I had never been gliding and said, "Oooohhh!" He arranged and paid for me to do a gliding flight. It was such fun, I loved it and the instructor he had arranged for me was great. I really enjoyed the experience and to this day I remember him and his kindness to me.

***

Chapter 38
Papua New Guinea (PNG)

I saw an advertisement for the Civil Aviation Authority in Papua New Guinea (PNG). Imagine me working for the bad guys—the regulators? No way. But apply I did, and off to PNG, I went. Silly me, I was quite confident I could handle PNG. I had lived in Angola, Burundi and some other suspect countries. During my time in Angola, the civil war was ongoing. In Burundi, there was gunfire every night. I can handle PNG I thought. The ex-CAA officer whom I was replacing said no place on earth is worse than PNG. Well, how right he was, at least amongst the places I have been. Accommodation was great; I lived in a hotel apartment—very nice. Everyone was so nice. But that was surface stuff. In reality it really was the most dangerous place I have lived.

***

I had decided to do a law degree in place of a social life. When I was not working, I filled my time with study—excellent, I learnt. I learnt what a clown I had been during my divorce when I had tried to be fair, just got my head kicked in. Man or woman, when it comes to divorce, you should go in boots and all because if you don't, the one trying to be seen as fair ends up being taken to the cleaners, as the other side thinks you are weak. Whereas if you fight your side, in maybe five years when the dust has settled, there is a good chance you could be friends, as there is no animosity about the foul play one has been subjected too. Anyway, that is my belief; let's get back on track. PNG is such a beautiful country, but so full of rascals.

I have lived amongst many cultures and the one thing I have come to realise that all cultures have their bogeymen. So, having been robbed at gunpoint, I rang a local lass who I had worked with and asked her who was the scary man in PNG culture. Amongst the indigenous Australians, it was the Kadaitcha man. In PNG, it came down to what area of PNG they came from. I thought that the young man was from the Mount Hagen area, when he had stolen my computer bag, he had also ended up with my aviation watch, my mobile and some worn underwear—as I had been on an overnight. So, having purchased a new phone, I rang the thief on my old phone and told him I was going to have him killed by the 'Sanguma man'.

He said, "You don't know any Sanguma men."

"Yes, I do, I have been in PNG nearly three years and I know how much it will cost me and how to contact them—so I am going to have you killed." After a bit of to and fro, I had reduced him to tears and he offered to meet me out by the university. I refused, I said "No you will kill me way out there, so I shall get someone to contact you." I rang my local friend back and asked her husband to take over. I got my computer back but didn't worry about my phone or watch, I just bought new ones. It cost me a little money but if you understand their culture, it can work to your advantage.

***

One Sunday, a colleague rang me, worried he was going to be killed. I had told my colleague and his wife that you should never get involved. Yes, you can give money but do not interfere in their lives. But his wife, whom I shall call Fiona, had a bubbly personality and chatted to anyone. She had been out to Australia and on her return, she had met a young man whom she befriended. He was wanting to do a documentary about the head-hunters. So, she offered to help, took him home to Daryl and said, "Look what I have." Long and short of it, they had a contact with a local man who worked at the yacht club. They convinced him to help the documentary maker so the local man threw in his job at the yacht club and took the film man to Hagen to set off on a trek to meet the head-hunters. Once all the filming had been done, they returned to Port Moresby. But because the local man had lost his job at the yacht club, Daryl was being held accountable and they wanted pay back.

***

That very weekend, an expatriate had been bashed to death at his home right in the heart of Port Moresby, so Daryl was panic-stricken that the same would happen to him. So they rang me. While I really wanted to give Fiona a big, 'I told you so—don't get fucking involved', I kept quiet and went about telling him how to extradite himself from this problem. In these cultures, bashing to death is an extremely personal death and I knew of one other man in my time in the Islands that it had happened to.

I said to Daryl, "You must hang tough when they come with the local chief of police, which they were threatening. Get out your camera and take photos. Threaten back—the police will not interfere no matter what they are threatening you with. But they are not going to kill you, just blackmail you. They only kill you, if you are knocking off their girlfriends, or are a kiddie fiddler." As rumour had it, the victim of the bashing in Port Moresby was the latter. The other man whom I knew about, was having it off with a local man's girlfriend and he and the girl's father took matters into their own hands. Payback is immediate, and they consider us weak when we don't do the same. A female pilot before my time in PNG caught a taxi home; she was a little tipsy and rather than drive drunk she got a taxi. The driver took her to his village and the majority of males in that village raped her. The taxi driver then killed her. After serving a few years in prison he was let out and did the same again, only this time to a local lass. Payback happened. Killed by his own people. These people kill perpetrators; unless it is a white person they have killed or raped, they let the law take its natural course. If a local lass or child is harmed by a white person, they will be subjected to a death by bashing.

***

Being the CAA's test officer, I was often sent to outlying airports where the applicant sometimes needed to put me in a hotel or room in his house, whatever worked for them. On one occasion, I had to fly to New Brittan, an Island north of Port Moresby. On arrival, I was greeted by the test applicant and taken to his home to be billeted for the night, I met his wife and then I was given a tour of this beautiful island.

We dropped his wife back at home and we went to the airport to get the aircraft ready for tomorrow's flight test. There were some adolescents looking through the perimeter wire of the airport. They called me over and as I went to say hello, these young men all exposed themselves to me. The airport security guard was horrified and he ran to chase them off. I just laughed and said I had seen bigger dicks on dogs. He thought this was hilarious. I returned to my test candidate and thought no more of the matter. However, on my return to Moresby I was very surprised to find everyone knew. My direct boss said to me everyone is talking of your retort. Not sure what they found so fascinating as I thought no more of it.

***

On one trip I arrived at Kerima to be greeted by the agent telling me that there was a six-year-old in the local jail, who was being held for killing his sister. Now, the jail consisted of a cage of bars—no roof, no protection from weather and this six-year-old was being held there until the circuit judge came around. I enquired as to what had happened. There was an event in one of the villages in the high country. The parents decided they would go. When they go anywhere everyone from the smallest child to the oldest adult will carry their share of what is to be transported. He had been given his little sister to transport and as they traversed the terrain her blanket had got caught up around her face and under her nose and she suffocated. The police had gone up the river by canoe to arrest this little six-year-old to await trial. On arrival back at Moresby, I contacted my friend's daughter who had left PNG but still had knowledge of the system.

She told me whom to contact in the prosecutor's office. I rang the person in question who informed me they were a member of the prosecutor's staff and shouldn't be talking to me. However, I was to send an email to a private email address stating the facts as I knew them. The circuit judge was sent there approximately two weeks later and '*mens rea* and *actus reus*,' I had thought, might be factors. It had been this, I had pointed out to the person who had helped when I first made contact. I have no idea what happened or what factors were used but I received an email saying the young boy had been released and it was thought that there would be no further action. I believe this was the case. Death by misadventure, I believe the finding was. So, if I have achieved nothing else in my life, I think just that small act, a phone call, has been worth it all.

***

I used to go out approximately once every couple of weeks with a couple of friends to go to the Japanese restaurant in Port Moresby.

On one such night, there was a nasty incident on going home. Sandra was very pregnant and getting to the end of her pregnancy, so her husband used to drive her to our dinners. Jacq lived close by and I lived out near Seven Mile—that was the name of the suburb. We waited with Sandra in the car park until her husband arrived to pick her up. I followed them out as we lived in the same direction.

I was driving my car along the main road, which had overpasses in various areas to allow foot traffic to cross safely. As I approached, something caught my eye and I felt wary. So, I literally put my foot to the floor. I have been told I had the same sort of engine that the formula one drivers have—it had been a special edition. I have no idea but when you put your foot to the floor she jumped and lunged forward. I thought no more about this until the next day.

I received a phone call to say that Sandra and her husband had been rocked at one of the overpasses and their car had taken substantial damage. He had somehow fallen behind me in the traffic and had not noticed my sudden speed and they had copped three or four large very large rocks on to their bonnet and roof. Luckily, it missed their windscreen. He knows what would have awaited them had he stopped. He kept control of the car and kept going as fast as he could with the damage incurred. The rascals use to do this in the hope you would crash and then rob and murder you if you weren't already dead.

***

Another day, I was caught in traffic at a large roundabout when I saw three bodies lying in a row. The police had shot them as they tried to rob a local business. This was life in PNG. You took it in your stride—turned up for business one day and life went on. So, my law degree did its job; it kept me home and studying. You really took your life in your hands to go out at night.

***

I had a medical due and went to see the local doctor who was qualified to do aviation medicals. As we chatted, he asked many questions about learning to fly. He then told me of a friend who had just immigrated to Australia. Like him, the other doctor and his family were Asian. He told how his friend's young son had come home from school spouting that if his parents smacked him, he could report them to the police. When the young lad went off to school next day as he walked out the door, he saw a suitcase by the door waiting for him. His father told him that he would be sorry to lose his son but he understood that he would want to live where he was not chastised and he wished him happiness living with his teacher. The child immediately stopped and said, "You mean I can't live here anymore?"

Father just said, "My house, my rules. I only punish you when you are being rude, disrespectful or just plain naughty. If I cannot do that, then you must live with your teacher in her utopia." The young man picked up the suitcase and took it to his room, acknowledging Dad's right to be a father in his own home.

When I look and see the very rude behaviour of some younger people I think 'Good on Dad'.

***

The Twin Otter is known for some very dramatic approaches. I had been taught as soon as you were over the actual strip on a very short field, you should put the aircraft into reverse. The aircraft stops flying and you literally fallout of the sky. No problem if only inches off the runway /strip, however in places like PNG many pilots do this in order to get into difficult strips—strips located in amphitheatres and extremely short in length. I was actually with one pilot in Fiji—at the time, he showed me how it works. Most impressive—6000 feet one moment and circuit height the next, which should be 1000 feet above ground level (AGL). Fantastic manoeuvre—only one danger—if it doesn't come out of reverse, you are dead. I have never known of this to happen on an Otter. These manoeuvres were necessary as the locals learnt that when the aircraft appeared overhead and the windsock was showing an extremely windy wrong direction—the pilot would just leave without the scheduled arrival and departure occurring for that village. The villagers started weighing down the windsock. People died because this pilot would be approaching, only to find himself with a strong tailwind pushing him straight into the mountains. If he was lucky and managed to just crash without loss of life, then well done. But there would be no aircraft to get out with. On the short strip, quite often, it was not really long enough for departure. You would fly off the end and nose down into the valley gaining airspeed as you did. The aircraft as it reached flying speed, would then depart normally. All of these tricks were used and we became extremely good at handling. However, I am aware there was an Otter pilot who was promoted to a Dash 8, I believe this manoeuvre is possible on the old 100 series aircraft but any later model the aircraft would not recover. This pilot who had been moved to the new fleet was in extremely bad weather approaching Madang, the aircraft didn't recover as happened in PNG where I think 28 people died.

***

Another problem we experienced, was that a navigation aid would be put into an area to assist in navigation; these days GPS does much of the work. However, GPS approaches are not suitable everywhere. So, you would use the Non Directional Beacon (NDB) or the Very High Frequency Omni Radial (VOR) to fly an approach. Problem was that the locals would steal the copper wire and the aid wouldn't be working. Even in my last weeks in Moresby some rascals stole the copper wire off the main approach beacon for Port Moresby's main airport—the airport that Qantas and Air Niugini use, along with many other local operators.

It was great flying but the aircraft were not maintained well and I had my first incident, no one was hurt but I was very embarrassed. I was with a training captain whom was checking me into some new strips, we had done the checklist but the nose wheel tended to wander. It had been reported constantly over the last eight years and was signed off by engineers—no fault found. Different pilot, same problem—they just weren't fixing the faults. Anyway, too long must have elapsed between the landing and completing of checklist and touch down and the nose wheel had again wandered and we ran off the strip. In a normal airline company, the training captain would have been responsible, but I was white, he was local and I was the one punished.

I consider I was treated badly in this case. I decided to resign. I was approaching 70 at this time so I packed up and went home to Australia. I love my life; on arriving in Australia I was immediately offered employment instructing again with a chance to move up to CFI, to replace one who was about to retire. But I was working for a shonk and decided to move on. I didn't stay long there—too old to have to fight the battles all over again. This company worked some of the Islands and when the young pilots came in with their stories about poor maintenance etc., the blatant breaking of the rules, I decided I didn't want to be responsible for that mess.

Chapter 39
Diplomas in Bullying

After I left, I heard on the grapevine that CASA had caught up with them and they lost their Air Operators Certificate (AOC). They deserved it. So, I was foot-loose and fancy-free and just settling down and thinking of retirement when I was offered employment by a large Western Australia flying school. I had been staying in Cairns waiting for my unit to become vacant. While visiting my friend further north I had been staying the night when I slipped on the bathroom floor and broken my ankle, which was extremely bad and I needed to have an operation to fix it.

Once mobile again and with a new medical I was off to Western Australia. I met with the HR man and the CEO plus the Operations Manager. Also, the ex-Chief pilot—it seems he was too compliant to management and was allowing these men (the CEO and the Operations Manager) to pressure the instructors into breaking the rules. It seems the CEO was from a North American company but the gentleman himself was ex-Belgian military. The Operations Manager was a Singaporean helicopter pilot who had obviously not read the Australian rules regarding how many hours a pilot can fly. They assumed that the Australian instructors would be able to fly the same hours as the American instructors and of course they do a lot more hours. It does depend on the level of licence held, but for ATPL holders it is 1500 hours against 900 in Australia.

When the North American company had sent the then prospective CEO to examine the company and carry out due diligence, he was not very diligent and got it wrong—the hours flown, relationship with CASA, knowledge of the rules and regulations of the country the school is in. He had failed to do the homework associated with buying into such an organisation.

On arrival in WA, I started work immediately and had my interview with CASA, which went well. I was told I had walked into a 'can of worms' (an Australian expression meaning 'not good'). CASA laid out the problems—I was to ignore any assistance from the ex-CFI, whom they said flouted the rules and regulations and was so busy kissing arse he couldn't do his job. The ex-CFI greeted me as an old friend. He was a very strange man and on my first day showed me photos of his prepubescent daughters, naked running under a hose, having first asked me if I would like to see photos of his daughters. Now, little children maybe, but the eldest was obviously showing signs of puberty. He was also known to show photos of his wife getting out of the shower. I was a bit stunned at this. However later there were more disturbing reports from other staff. He had been in cohorts with both the CEO and the Operations Manager. Bullying was rife. They were feared. Getting the sack was a constant threat, my first job was to build some morale amongst the instructors and I started having pilots' nights, where I supplied the food and drinks and we just talked. They quickly realised I was not like their previous management. If I made a decision then I stood by it. I took the knocks.

The CEO very quickly made sure that I knew he was determined to bring those lazy Australians into line, however most of my instructors were New Zealanders and they were hard-working proficient men and women. He was out to make life as hard as possible for them. I spent much of my time taking the bastard apart. One of his decrees thought up by the Operations Manager was that when the students returned from an exercise, the instructor used to leave the aircraft at the refuelling bay and walk back to write up his or her report on how the exercise had gone—what the student needed to work on, good points they had achieved and a general synopsis of the lesson. The student without the instructor on board would then taxi the aircraft to the parking bays. One parking bay was a 15-second taxi and the other was 27 seconds. He claimed that not only were they being paid a bonus on the hours flown they were also cheating on hours. Hours in aviation are very important, as it is a sign of experience.

This was just one of the stupid ideas on how to a) save money and b) keep the instructors in line. I had great fun writing a letter to solve this problem, suggesting that the seconds involved were so many parts of a minute, which was so many parts of an hour—the end result being that we should not refuel after every flight when the fuelling bay was usually empty and refuelling was quick— the most with the other aircraft in front of you. My suggestion was that all twenty aircraft should refuel first thing in the morning. If each aircraft took 10 minutes to refuel then with 20 aircraft to be refuelled, the last aircraft would be three hours and 20 minutes late departing. I never did hear any more about the pilots ripping off the company. So funny. They both had diplomas in stupidity. He would bark at me saying I was only flying so many hours a month in a school of this size but CASA wanted me to be on the ground with just the occasional sortie. In a school this size, it is the running of the management that one must see to. Instead, I spent my time writing letters to this cretin trying to keep us legal, get the hours flown and generally run a tight profitable school. The frustration was enormous and I was swearing once again but boy I wrote a good letter. This happened more than once, I seemed to spend much of my time keeping this pair of rabid individuals in check. Going with instructors to hearings of supposed infractions was constant, the stupidity of these men, was monumental.

He did make it hard—I am pleased to say I got the sack for gross misconduct. What a laugh! All the students went on strike—they got drunk and couldn't fly because they were protesting my dismissal. I couldn't have cared less except that they were going to get out of paying me my entitlements. So, I took them to Fairwork Australia and also departed on my holiday that had been previously booked. I was informed by Fairwork Australia that the hearing was to be held while I was on holiday. I was actually going to theatre in the UK and then leaving for France, Barcelona and other parts of Europe. They told me the date and time (WA time) and I looked at my itinerary and found I would be in France. I bought myself a French sim card, sent them the phone number and was informed of the time I would be rung, in order for me to be online and ready before the adjudicator arrived.

I had contacted people who had suffered the same fate as me and was given permission to give their names and address, phone numbers, anything that would help if required to prove my point. After 45 minutes, the adjudicator asked me to hang up as he wanted to speak to the company out of my hearing. He would ring me back in twenty minutes he said.

He did ring and his first words were, "If you lose this today will you appeal to the ATT?" which is the equivalent of the Federal High Court.

"Yes," I said.

He replied, "Good." He said he had never seen such a blatant case of wrongful dismissal. He said he had told them to go and have a discussion amongst themselves, as in his view I had been exonerated. If they didn't come to some satisfactory settlement, he would recommend me to go the ATT. He asked me to supply the names of the nine others whom had been treated so badly so he could contact them as he was going to take this matter further. He did. The CEO got deported. God bless his little cotton socks. What happened to the Operations Manager? He was hired by CASA (told you it was staffed by incompetent losers).

The adjudicator rang me back to say that they had backed off and I would be paid my entitlements and that I was no longer guilty of gross misconduct. During this time, I owe a great big thank you to Graeme and his wife Anne (a great cook.) They took me in when I had to leave company quarters and stored my belongings. They made my 70th birthday cake—fantastic.

So, what had I done that was so dreadful? Well the CEO and the Operations Manager had bullied a young instructor so badly he was left cowering in a corner and had to be coaxed out by his immediate superior as he had become afraid of these men. This particular instructor was not a favourite of mine but I went to bat for him and would do so again in an instant.

He was crouched down in the corner. I was contacted and immediately wrote an email to the head of the *ab initio* flying conducted at the other base. I simply said what has happened is assault. Assault does not have to be hands on; it just has to be where you make someone afraid for their safety. This young man had been clearly assaulted and the next time it happened he was to call the police. I still have a copy of that email. I was, according to the charge against me regarding my dismissal, 'inciting discord'.

At the hearing, the HR man presented the company's side. "Call the police—really?"

No wonder when asked by the adjudicator regarding what did I want from the hearing I said just what I am owed. I didn't want my job back, as going to work was like entering a war zone daily. I would know, I had been in war zones.

Chapter 40
Back to the East Coast of Oz

On returning from my overseas holiday, I decided to return to Brisbane and look for a job. My mother had gone into a care home while I had been in Western Australia. She had actually gone into hospital for a small operation and while there, she had fallen, breaking her shoulder, which meant she could no longer care for herself as she was in her nineties. They operated and at 93 they gave her a new shoulder. The operation went well but she never again gained her independence as she was already disabled and this put an end to her mobility.

I was asked to a central Queensland town to become the CFI of a flying school there. I was working for a company of god botherers—the most dreadful company I have come across. They wouldn't pay bills till the last minute, and gave dreadful service. It was run by the son of an American-type minister, who claimed in the Church of England or Roman Catholic churches, he would be a canon. This guy had never been ordained and he, by declaring it a missionary organisation, ran tax-free. Never once was there a trip of a missionary nature—sheer hogwash.

His son whom was my Grade 3 instructor, would not work weekends as he played sport and went to church. He would not write up lesson reports and I couldn't put students up for their first solo flights without correct paperwork. He would argue asking where it was written he had to provide paperwork regarding progress tests. Grade 2 instructors are allowed to send solo but not Grade 3, they can do the training—giving lessons regarding rules and regulations etc. But it was and still is considered that they do not have the judgement to send solo. So, I was stuck with this belligerent little arsehole, who wanted to know where whatever I said was written. I stayed eight weeks. It's okay to talk the talk but if you don't walk the walk then I am not interested. Here was this family ripping off the Australian tax office, the students and in general not living what they espoused in their religion. I say again, I hate god-botherers and do-gooders with a passion.

I was out of work for five minutes again and I was thinking of hanging up my headphones when I got offered a job 100 meters away. Their CFI was off on holidays, he confided to me that he was desperately looking for work. He wanted bigger, he wanted out. What I didn't know was that they (the company) wanted him gone too.

I took over on a temporary basis and was enjoying the work, had been given a student who was having problems with diversions etc. Another guy had just purchased a very nice Baron and needed to be endorsed in this type of aircraft. When the test officer came up from another state, as I didn't have testing approval at this school, he passed both so I was quite pleased with them. At the end of my tenure the other CFI had returned and I was told he had spoken with management but I had not spoken to him. I was asked to lunch by management by way of thank you. At the lunch, I was informed that the CFI was moving on. I immediately thought he had been successful in his search for new employment. So, when offered his position, I said yes. Next thing, I received a very angry text from CFI accusing me of being a low-down skunk. Apparently, he hadn't resigned—he had been fired. While I was being wined and dined, he was being given his walking papers. OOPS! However, I know he landed on his feet and got a far better job so good on him. I was happy there, I liked the people, the atmosphere, the training and all went well. I did have some problems though. I started to become impatient and found my fuse when dealing with stupidity and inefficiency, even shorter than it had been before. I was by now approaching 73 and handed in my resignation, as I had things to do in life. I had one student whom I still like immensely and wrote to him the other day to ask if I could use him in this book. He very kindly said yes, as not all I have to say about teaching him is nice.

I also found working in a small-town frustrating—people become important in their own minds and bully you instead of working with you. One of their airport workers in one of the little yellow cars thought he was tough. I asked him a question one day, regarding when the airport would be able to open. There had been a cyclone and some areas of the airport had flooded. He said they were doing the best they could and who was I to question him. My request had been polite, I had already talked to the tower and here was this goose overriding the tower. I did take CASA on regarding new rules they brought in and through the local politician it went to the senate and we won. But did they fix the situation having been ordered to? No, they blamed air services and air services blamed CASA and that situation still stands today.

Chapter 41
Instructing

How do you teach people to learn how to fly? I have always tried to make them feel safe and tell them it is easy. It is easy, once they learn not to fight with the aircraft.

I have met the wankers who only want to learn to impress the girls and I have met those who don't believe that I, a woman, can possibly be working in aviation. I think many of those attitudes have now changed. I remember going to a party in the UK and I was introduced to this man with, "Oh, this is Lesley and she is an FO for the company I am working for."

This short, fat tub of lard said, "OH YEAH, pigs might fly."

I quickly retorted saying, "Sir, you are clear for take-off." He had such a big arse; I am sure that is where he kept his brains.

Then in Australia another man told me he had to take over from his female instructor. Problem is I call these people out. I am not polite about it either.

But apart from that sort of response I have had great fun teaching both ground and flight training and most times I have been successful in getting the message through. Yes, I have had failures—there was an extremely nice young man who had an alcohol problem—he was hoping to better himself in life. Unfortunately, the alcohol won and he dropped out.

I did feel for him as he was trying so hard. He had a hard life and instead of curling up and giving in, he was trying and I thought that was sad. Another was a lady who came to me with some 60 hours and hadn't gone solo. She flew extremely well, just couldn't land it, every time she would be on approach, she would just keep flying into the ground. Never once did she try to flare (which is a slight alteration of the nose attitude to stop flying into the ground). Every time, the same—a crash landing would be imminent if the instructor hadn't stepped in. It didn't matter how I tried; it was always such an over correction. Now, with nose high, such a sudden alteration in nose attitude can cause the aircraft to stall (a stall in an aircraft is not like in a car where the engine stops. In an aircraft it is the breakup of laminar airflow over the wing and subsequent decrease in lift with resultant nose drop). In the end, I moved away and someone else inherited this lady. On our last debrief, she told me she flew on instruments and couldn't understand why she couldn't land on instruments. I believe it was another 30 hours before she went solo. She was good, just didn't fly looking outside the aircraft. There was another man, 60 hours and not solo. His instructor at another school had in desperation sent him to me. I got him solo in half an hour. The other instructor had taught him well but the guy over controlled.

I said in very plain English, "You know Frank if you had to wank that hard it would come off in your hand."

He went very red but got the message and the next landing was a bit heavy but safe, another two reasonable landings and he was sent solo. Such great jubilation from him and his instructor. A lot of my students and I became friends and we are still in contact. Ian was another student—a real cheeky man and still is to this day. He and his wife visit me, even after all these years.

He was flying extremely well—conditions good and I said as encouragement, "Make this a good one and you can go solo."

He said, "Give me a kiss and I will."

My response was quick and bloody, "To go to bed with you, I would have to be too lazy to masturbate. Just land it and stop mucking around." He broke up completely, and still laughing, pulled off the nicest landing and he was solo.

I also endorsed Ian in a Mooney M20 and these aircraft are notorious at the stall. Wing drop, snap roll resulting in a spin that can be hard to recover from due to the extremely small rudder and large tail plane/elevator. They can enter a flat spin and they are almost impossible to get out of. We were lucky it was a dynamic spin and it came out with spin recovery technique. Ian said it was the only time he ever heard me swear in an aircraft. On the ground, upset me, frustrate me, and I let fly, but in the air never. I just don't do it.

I laughed about being rung by CAA for low flying. I was supposed to have gone below 500 feet, which was our lower limit in the training area. I hadn't, but the aircraft had really large letters of the call sign under the wing, as do all aircraft, but in this aircraft the letters were very much larger than usual. Having talked my way out of that incident I was doing circuits with a student when we got hit by a golf ball. There was a driving range at the end of the airport runway 31 at Moorabbin many years ago. There went my low flying excuse.

I even failed a Qantas captain who violated controlled airspace. He was bored with the big ones and wanted to do a little personal flying. We went on a small sortie and he flew well. But he was about to clip the edge of controlled airspace when I stepped in. My boss in those times was called Gary and Gary said, "Sorry mate, if she said you fail you fail."

He went on saying, "I would bet she gave you three warnings, didn't she? Let's review your flight on nearing Pakenham—did she point out the 4000-foot step? As you approached Caribbean Gardens, did she say casually about the line that is between Mt Dandenong and the Gardens, plus the police academy on the hill, all at the very edge of the control zone?" The very sheepish captain admitted I had. Gary god bless his little cotton socks, sorted the situation and the following week the guy came back and I signed him off.

One of my last students was an English man, a big man—an ex-Paratrooper. I actually think he was in the SAS, although he would never say. I used to have to look up at him, he was an extremely strong man, large and solid. He was enthusiastic but so heavy handed and I trotted out my, "Seduce it, don't rape it;

if you wank that hard, it will come off in your hand." Most of the vulgarities usually shock them and then sink in. A large circuit with me will get the comment of, "This isn't a navigation exercise—I haven't bought a picnic lunch—tighten the circuit."

John actually said to me one day, "You have insulted me today and been rude to me."

My comment back was, "I am always rude to people who don't listen—you are costing yourself money and that is stupid—so that makes you stupid."

I would have hit me but he just grinned and said, "You can't get rid of me like that—I have lots of money and I don't care—just book me another lesson." But his English accent was known on the airport and one of the controllers came from John's neck of the woods in the UK. Dave, the controller, said to me, "he hasn't gone solo."

"No," I said, "he doesn't understand gentle, I have tried all the 'seduce it, don't rape it' scenarios."

Dave who was also a commercial pilot said, "Tell him to touch it like he would touch another man's dick."

I was rather shocked. "I can't say that." But during another lesson where he just about tore the wings off, I said to him, "Dave in the tower told me to say this—you should fly the aircraft like you would touch another man's dick." John went solo that day. The penny dropped. He has since gone on, bought his own aircraft and flies around Australia, has done a private instrument rating and no longer fights with his aircraft.

I admit my teaching technique is different—I talk to them on a level they understand. It is not just about taking money for the flight, it is about relating, making sure they understand aerodynamics principles of flight and how to correct situations. Flying in shitty weather, as you may depart in 8 Oktas (the sky is divided into eighths these eighths are called Oktas and cloud is given in Oktas) 8/8 is overcast, you may have departed in Cavok (another aviation term) but departing in blue skies only to find the arrival airport's weather has deteriorated. It is most important before that licence is issued that you know how to cope.

Circuit height is 1000'AGL but better to do a circuit at 800'AGL than to enter low cloud. There is so much more to instructing but that is how I have done it and all of my students are still alive.

I have now retired and I don't really miss it. I guess it was something I loved so passionately, and to see people make it so hard, frustrated me so badly I was getting ratty. I realised it was time to bow out gracefully, having had the most wonderful life. I've seen the world and contributed in some small way to people's lives.

When I look back, I have been very lucky, had a wonderful life and it has been an honour to have worked with the people I have.

Chapter 42
Why France

I always loved English theatre and after I retired (one month after turning 73), I had decided to go backpacking, starting in the UK and going to some shows, then on to wherever. When my mother, who was approaching ninety-six years old, suddenly deteriorated, I stayed until she passed. I looked at my situation in Australia. I love Australia, but did not just want to become another veggie and just exist. There was nothing for me in Australia except family who didn't want to know me. So, I departed with no real plan in mind. I ended up in France close enough to the UK for me to go and see theatre and friends but not have that dreadful UK weather. After being hassled by our social security about what I was doing when I was returning to Australia, I decided to purchase an old home and renovate it myself. Funny thing is, now I am here, I cannot afford the theatre on my pension. I have got older and the work has taken longer than I thought. But hopefully now it is almost finished, I will be able to sell it and return to Australia.

Epilogue

The name I almost called this book was 'care factor zilch' but decided it would give the wrong impression. So, I have changed my mind once again and called it 'Up there' as that is where life is most fun. But in truth, many people will think I have made light of serious situations. But it is humour that keeps us doing the job. It is not because I, and the people who I worked with, don't care. If we didn't care, we wouldn't have been there—sometimes putting ourselves in danger. But you can care too much and this makes you vulnerable to the rogues and rascals. Emotion can cloud judgement. Better to save who we can rather than risk life and limb, trying to save the world. So, we never talk about it and we give the impression of not giving a shit. In actuality we are professionals doing the job we are employed to do and such remarks as, "Tell someone who cares," or, "tell it to the padre," are simply bravado and a way of deflecting praise or negative remarks. However, if I had the chance to do it all over again, I would, in a heartbeat. I love my life.